WELCOME TO THE
Other Side!

RECLAIMING LIFE AFTER SURVIVING AND CAREGIVING THROUGH THE ABYSS OF CANCER

Sherri and John Snoad

BALBOA.PRESS
A DIVISION OF HAY HOUSE

Balboa Press books may be ordered through booksellers or by contacting:

Balboa Press
A Division of Hay House
1663 Liberty Drive
Bloomington, IN 47403
www.balboapress.com
844-682-1282

Because of the dynamic nature of the Internet, any web addresses or links contained
in this book may have changed since publication and may no longer be valid. The views
expressed in this work are solely those of the author and do not necessarily reflect the
views of the publisher, and the publisher hereby disclaims any responsibility for them.

The author of this book does not dispense medical advice or prescribe the use of any
technique as a form of treatment for physical, emotional, or medical problems without the
advice of a physician, either directly or indirectly. The intent of the author is only to offer
information of a general nature to help you in your quest for emotional and spiritual well-
being. In the event you use any of the information in this book for yourself, which is your
constitutional right, the author and the publisher assume no responsibility for your actions.

Any people depicted in stock imagery provided by Getty Images are models,
and such images are being used for illustrative purposes only.
Certain stock imagery © Getty Images.

Print information available on the last page.

ISBN: 978-1-9822-7250-0 (sc)
ISBN: 978-1-9822-7249-4 (hc)
ISBN: 978-1-9822-7248-7 (e)

Library of Congress Control Number: 2021915723

Balboa Press rev. date: 08/26/2021

To all the patients, survivors and caregivers in the world who have ever found themselves lost in the stormy seas of cancer and recovery, this book is dedicated to you. May it be the lighthouse that guides you to the friendly shores of life after cancer.

CONTENTS

INTRODUCTION

The title of *survivor* is a badge being issued to more and more people today. This title means victory and life. But even though you have an enormous sense of pride at overcoming the odds and obstacles, the term *survivor* causes you to continually revisit the struggle or trauma that made you the survivor. Likewise, when someone is dubbed *caregiver*, that implies a position of helping the seriously ill. Once you have earned these titles, you may feel constrained, even trapped, preventing you from moving on and being who you are supposed to be as a thriving human being. It is difficult to live a fulfilling life when one is forced to live in the past, imprisoned by a title.

The number of people affected by cancer is astounding. Both the National Cancer Institute and the American Cancer Society have done conclusive research and found nearly 40 percent of men and more than 37 percent of women will be diagnosed with some form of cancer in their lifetimes. This also means there are just as many, and conceivably more, caregivers than diagnosed patients, making the combined cancer patient and caregiver population substantial. Of course, the exciting news here is that more and more are earning the title of *survivor* than ever before, and with advances in science, these numbers will continue to increase. Life after cancer needs to be candidly talked about now more than ever. This growing fellowship of survivors and their caregivers has to find safe passage to the other side of illness and recovery.

Much has been documented and published about cancer and treatment. Yet, an often-overlooked aspect of cancer is what happens in recovery. Recovery can last a lifetime, and there is no road map. Everyone's road through recovery is as unique as their cancer. However easy or difficult, recovery deserves as much attention as the disease itself. Imagine jumping out of a plane, but no one showed you how to open your parachute for a safe landing. That was how it felt for us—and how it feels for millions more like us. Survival is filled with real, everyday challenges, both emotional and physical.

We all travel different paths prior to a diagnosis as a cancer patient or being enlisted as a caregiver. When the cancer train pulls into the station, we all arrive with our past experiences, including our strengths and even our baggage that has accumulated. Though we may come from different places, backgrounds, and experiences, we all now ride the same train. The commonalities we share once the journey of patient, survivor, and caregiver begins is universal.

The James Cancer Hospital at the Ohio State University Medical Center, where Sherri underwent treatment, invited cancer patients, survivors, and their caregivers to a concert about hope featuring singer-songwriter Melissa Ethridge. It was a special, emotionally charged afternoon. Melissa Etheridge told her moving breast cancer survivor story between the heartfelt songs she performed. All of us were there to celebrate life, hope, and strength.

Her final song was a special one she wrote called "I Run for Life." She had penned this cancer anthem when she herself was diagnosed. The lyrics deeply touched everyone, so much so that by the last verse and refrain, there was not a dry eye in the place. Every cheek had tears freely flowing. The power of this moment was incredible as we looked around and felt as if we all were one.

It didn't matter if you were in treatment or in recovery, whether just a few years out or many, everyone—even the caregivers—was crying. The tears weren't about the song; in that moment, everyone was reliving their own personal fight. When you are diagnosed with something like cancer, there is a special bond with everyone else who has experienced it. Deep down, we are all the same. Each person there fought a different version of the same fight, but we were all warriors united on the same team.

The story of patient-survivor and caregiver is full of intertwining, yet different parallel experiences. If cancer were a pair of eyeglasses to be shared, it was as if we were looking through two totally different lenses. Though our journey may have been together, how each interpreted and coped often differed.

In this story, we share the myriad obstacles faced after cancer, some of which are often avoided in open conversation. With candid and open conversation, we provide a resource for anyone impacted by a similar life-changing event. We'll explore difficult issues like socializing with others again, overcoming triggers that create paralyzing fear and anxiety, regaining independence from science and medicine, survivors' guilt, the search for normalcy, intimacy, and sex, and other topics. This ride we are about to take you on is told as a dual narrative, with the two unique perspectives of illness and recovery, helping survivors and caregivers alike find inspiration to forge ahead, knowing there is hope on the other side.

PART I

AND THIS HAPPENED

CHAPTER 1A: SHERRI

There's Somethin' Happenin' Here

From Cough to Cancer: How It All Went Down

Breathe. In, out, in, out.
Pump your arms!
Look ahead. Make it to that tree!
Keep moving your legs!
Here comes a car. Don't look like you're about to keel over!

Running is so much fun. Even though it can be a drudgery at times, running is joyous to me. It is a beautiful thing to be able to open the door and head out on an adventure. Running is empowering, and it fills me with strength and confidence. It is a natural high. Having spent my adult life as a nurse, a massage therapist, and a big believer in holistic health, I embrace the intrinsic value of exercise and staying fit—and all the good that goes along with it.

Something Is Not Right

Training for a half-marathon, I was scheduled to run eight miles on a Saturday in February. A week earlier, I noticed a tickle in my throat and a very slight cough. Perhaps I was coming down with something, maybe a slight cold. Yet another typical Ohio winter day—drab, cold, damp, and near freezing—I was five miles into the run when the coughing began. It went from bad to worse in just a few strides. The cough became violent. I couldn't breathe and staggered to the side of the road. I fell to my knees, coughing so hard it made me vomit. After calming myself, I ran, and coughed, all the way home, not knowing it would be my last run for a long time. Over the course of the next several days, the coughing persisted, and I scheduled a visit with my family physician.

Enter Modern Medicine

The doctor put me on a basic antibiotic and told me to monitor my cough. She was thinking perhaps either pneumonia or bronchitis. Antibiotics over the course of a week, along with rest, should have made a difference, but the cough did not get better. The antibiotic did not work. The doctor amped up the treatment with another antibiotic, steroids, and an inhaler. Still with no improvement, a chest x-ray was finally ordered by a doctor filling in for mine at the time. This substitute doctor, like my primary doctor, was thinking about pneumonia.

March 21: A Special Day

Ah, spring! March 21 generally marks the first day of spring and the excited anticipation of warmer days coming. For John and me, that date is even more special. The day you give birth to a child is a date you will always remember. Having twins makes the date doubly special. Our identical twin boys were born on March 21, and this was their twenty-second birthday. But March 21 also happens to be the day that the phrase "Sherri, you have cancer" came into my life. Needless to say, I definitely enjoyed the March 21 when the twins were born—much more than the March 21 that marked the end of my life as I knew it.

The Call That Changed Everything

On the line, the "substitute" doctor was telling me there was an abnormal-sized nodule in my lungs that looked like it may be cancer. At that moment, my heart skipped a beat, and my world came to a screeching halt. You know how directors freeze a moment in time for a character in a film? That happened in real life. The doctor informed me a CT scan was scheduled for the next day

Hope remained high for good news—until the doctor told me I could either come into her office or she could tell me on the phone what the CT results were. OK, that's not good. She certainly didn't want me to come to her office so she could shake my hand and say, "Congratulations. You have the best set of lungs I've ever seen."

There was no way I could wait for an appointment. "Tell me now."

And out came the words: "It looks like you have lung cancer."

Frozen in the moment, my mind raced. Whoa! How is that possible? I never smoked, I exercise regularly, and I eat healthy. Inside, my brain screamed, "WTF!"

The doctor claimed nothing more was known and was referring me to a cardiothoracic surgeon who specialized in lung cancer.

Reeling with emotion, especially with anger toward that doctor, I thought, *How could she offer to tell me this news over the phone?* I didn't remember or care that actually I had asked for the news.

The need to blame someone provided me distraction me from the real issue: that I might have cancer. She gave me this horrible news, and now I despised her. I would carry this anger toward her for a long time, but the reality of it was that she helped save my life, and I will forever be grateful.

Telling people such devastating news must be an awful part of being a doctor. I am fairly certain there is no course in medical school called "Destroying Someone's Life 101." Today, I have nothing but gratitude for her. About two years after treatment, on a whim, I stopped by the office and asked to speak to the doctor who helped save my life. In that moment, the bitterness and anger I carried inside were released. In tears, I thanked her for having a role in saving my life. Facing the demon that I had created— and admitting this anger was misplaced—was a powerful healing moment. Releasing this anger needed to occur for deep healing to be achieved.

The Waiting Game

"Wait and worry" seemed to be the repeating theme during the painfully long four-month process to get a definitive diagnosis. Being alone was not good for me. My mind was paralyzed by fear, making it impossible to distinguish between the reality of what I was dealing with and what my mind perceived or created. Fear generates frightening scenarios. Continuing to work and staying busy was a welcome distraction

At work, I wore my professional mask to hide the fear and stress that were raging inside. People around me would talk and laugh or discuss movies, their kids, their favorite restaurants, the fun things in life. I just wanted to scream, "Shut up! Just shut up with all this unimportant crap!" I would sit at my desk and think, *Something is wrong with me, and no one knows what it is.* Instead of letting my feelings show, I politely smiled or laughed and conversed as though my world wasn't falling apart.

Deep in my heart, I knew something was wrong because the bouts of coughing, often violent, continued. Coughing interrupted everything: talking, working, laughing, even sleeping at night. Lying flat would send me into a full-bodied "shake the bed" coughing fit (sadly, that was the only shaking our bed did during that time). I had to sleep propped up on pillows to help provide marginal relief. Sometimes I left and went to one of the spare bedrooms just so John could get some sleep.

It's Not Lung Cancer!

After a spring break trip to a warmer climate, where my symptoms lessened, and I actually felt improved, it was finally the moment of truth: the long-awaited appointment with the lung cancer surgeon. The trip infused me with hope since I felt better, but the dreaded cough was back. Sitting in the waiting room, observing everyone around us, we noticed their skin was pallid with tones of grays and yellows, sunken cheeks, and many gasping on oxygen. Most looked as if they were knocking on death's door. This shocked and frightened me, but at the same time, it gave me comfort. Surely, I don't have lung cancer because I'm not like them! And yet, what if I do? Will I become like them? Are my days numbered?

The cardiothoracic cancer surgeon cut right to the chase. A battery of tests and a biopsy were needed and scheduled to determine what was going on, marking the first of many physical scars I now wear.

Two weeks after that initial consultation, we reported to the James Cancer Hospital, aka "The James," at the Ohio State University's Wexner Medical Center. The cycle of being scanned and tested, followed by the agonizing wait time for results, would become a normal part of my life (though I didn't know it at the time). The biopsy results revealed a fungal infection—not lung cancer! I cried tears of joy at the doctor's office! That was the first sigh of relief in months. Now the torch would be passed to a new doctor; a referral was made to see an infectious disease doctor, shutting the door on a cancer diagnosis. Or so I thought.

Self-Advocacy Matters

We met with the infectious disease doctor. He was very clinical, methodical, and extremely data driven, which was difficult for me to relate to since I was desperately in need of reassurance and comfort. His demeanor was so stoic that I was ready to see a different doctor. Eventually, I would come to have an immense respect and gratefulness for his methodical expertise as he indeed had a large hand in saving my life. Speaking up is a necessity, and it was the first of many lessons we learned when navigating the medical system. Talk to your team! Ask questions about everything! All the scans and tests may reveal what's going on inside, but they can't see all the confusion, fear, and questions rolling around inside your head. Doctors are not mind readers, and we found out early on how important it is to communicate any questions or concerns.

A Random Call

Eating lunch at work in late May, I got an unexpected call from the cardiothoracic lung cancer surgeon. He asked how I was doing. I really was feeling quite well and was in a good place mentally. I was so surprised to hear from him. He said he was thinking of me and was glad to hear I was doing so well, but he wanted to do one more CT scan to verify all was well. He didn't have to do this, but he did not want me to "fall between the cracks" and be forgotten without another checkup. You would think this would have scared me beyond measure, but I was feeling so good that I didn't have an ounce of concern. I was so sick of procedures, but what was one more? I agreed to the scan.

The results hit me like a ton of bricks: another heart-stopping moment! It was utterly shocking. To everyone's surprise, instead of having just one nodule, my lungs were riddled with nodules! None of us could believe it. Clinically, even he noted that I looked better than the last time he had seen me, and I was emphatic that I had been feeling better. There was no reason to believe the antifungal meds were not doing the job.

When in the moment, or the middle of a crisis, sometimes we don't realize that the small, simple kindnesses make all the difference. This one little call to check on me was so above and beyond a surgeon's normal protocol, and it was so kind. He undoubtedly played a large role in saving my life.

Return to Fear

Back to full-on panic mode. How could this be? Even the cough had subsided since taking the antifungal meds. Clearly, I was getting better, right? On June 13, a new collection of "badges" was added to my body. Scars number two, three, and four were caused by a "wedge section" biopsy where a piece of my lung, in the area containing the nodule, was removed and sent for testing. A chest tube was inserted to drain fluid and prevent lung collapse. We now had to wait for word on the biopsy results.

When the World Comes to a Halt: An Alternate Reality

People who have had cancer are able to recall, often with great emotion, the vivid memory of the moment in time when they were told those three heart-stopping, jaw-dropping words: "You have cancer." From that moment on, life as you know it changes forever. What follows is my version of when those words were said to me.

While lying in a hospital bed, with my husband, John, next to me, after a lung biopsy in what became my first overnight stay, the cardiothoracic surgeon came into the room and removed the chest tube he had installed during surgery. After skillful removal of the tube, he moved to the foot of the bed and proceeded to tell us that I had a rare form of lymphoma. Oddly, I don't recall my reaction to this devastating news. Yet, my next memory is my oncology doctor standing at the foot of the bed next to the cardiothoracic surgeon and explaining that we needed to cancel our family trip to Europe, which was a week away, because the plan was to start treatment right away. With all that has happened since, I had never really thought about or reflected much on that day. What you just read is what replays over and over in my mind when I think about getting diagnosed.

My reality had been totally disrupted, and my world had been rocked. John and I wrote our versions of this chapter in the book totally separate from each other. Later, when we shared our work, and I read his interpretation of events, it was like reading someone else's story! Most of what he said was news to me, and I was learning about it for the first time.

According to John, the diagnosis came via a phone call from the cardiothoracic surgeon while we were at home. John took the call and offered to place it on speaker, but I refused. Our son Brian was next to me, and I stood crying in the kitchen as John and the doctor discussed the lymphoma diagnosis. There is no memory of this for me whatsoever. We had never really talked about the day I was diagnosed, so he had no idea about my version of the day.

This complete discrepancy between my memory and the reality of what happened was like living in an alternate universe. It was a mind-blowing experience. I later discovered cancer patients can experience a form of post-traumatic stress disorder (PTSD). My brain, in trying to protect itself, decided to "wall off" this traumatic memory and create a gentler way to process the memory. My mind created a memory that was comfortable to tell, almost like a scene out of TV medical drama, a memory that would not be as traumatizing to me every time I told it.

You Have Lymphoma. Just Say It: Cancer.

The doctor gave us the news. I had stage 3 non-Hodgkin's lymphomatoid granulomatosis. He said they believed it "may" have been caused by the Epstein-Barr virus, the same virus that causes mononucleosis. Supposedly, it was dormant in my system. For most people, the virus is present but kept at bay by a healthy immune system. For reasons we will never know, my system went, for lack of a better term, completely haywire. This form of lymphoma is actually quite rare.

All I heard was "lymphoma." *I have cancer?* Numbing shock set in. In just six days, we were supposed to be on a plane to Germany to visit our oldest, along with his wife, who was stationed in Germany for the US Army. It was to be a college graduation gift for our twin sons and a family reunion, together again as a family.

A moment is all it takes for the world to stop on a dime. In an instant, my life changed forever. I was carrying something in my body that could take my life. Thrust into the ring, I was now in a boxing match for my life. The team in my corner was rapidly being assembled. My husband was there for me every step of the way as my voice, my ears, and my rock to hold me up. The fact that I was a nurse became meaningless. Now a patient, thinking calmly and clinically went right out the door. I was numb, in denial but ready to fight.

Lessons Learned

1. Do *not* go to your appointments alone. If you don't have family nearby, ask a friend or a neighbor, but take someone with you as an advocate. This is important because you need to have a set of objective ears. Trust me on this. You will not hear things the way they are said. Your mind will twist it and turn it, and you may walk out of there thinking you need to make funeral plans.

2. Take notes. You can do it if you want, but have the person with you take them as well. They will be in a better state mentally to take accurate notes. Between appointments, put questions you have for your doctor down on paper, so when you go to the appointment, your list of questions is right in front of you. Often the conversation gets sidetracked, and you walk out forgetting to ask something you wanted to inquire about.

3. *You* matter. Your medical staff sees tons of people, more in one day than they probably would like. Don't settle with being a number. Be persistent. Make *you* matter to them. How, you ask? See number 4.

4. Be a squeaky wheel, because as the old saying goes, it is the squeaky wheel that gets the grease. In this case, ask questions and be insistent that you receive answers. Again, your doctor cannot read your mind. If you need something, say something. Your quality of life hangs in the balance—if not your life itself. After all, they are working for you!

5. Seek other opinions. If you feel your questions are not being answered or the level of care you are receiving is lacking, don't be afraid to get another opinion. It is your right and your life.

6. Stay off "Dr. Google." There are ways to do research, and there are ways not to. Just like your ears in the doctor's office, your mind will see what your subconscious mind tells it to. You will fall victim to thinking you have every disease known to man. It will do you no good.

7. Start a journal. Make notations on whatever form of calendar you use. Note everything from the science to the care received to the

instructions when you are discharged. And don't forget those little random things that were dwarfed at the time by all the procedures and science—like the cardiothoracic surgeon who just wanted to make sure I didn't slip through the cracks. Maybe you noted an unexpected visitor or received a small kind gesture from a nurse or volunteer. Reading these stories now fills my heart with all the wonderful people who helped me make it through.

CHAPTER 1B: JOHN

What the Hell Is Happening Here?

And This Happened

Life is a funny animal. Just when things are going your way, suddenly they aren't. When life takes a 180-degree turn, and suddenly you are staring at a crisis, will you be ready? Trust me, I never saw an obstacle that I did not believe could be overcome. Never. Until that one day when the news rocked my world and made me question everything.

That day started like any other early summer day, but the news came like a tornado and turned everything upside down. Sherri, my soul mate, wife, and best friend, was diagnosed with cancer. Cancer? Are you kidding me? My world began to spin wildly out of control, and as it spun faster and faster, the ground fell out from below my feet. I felt helpless, and for the first time in my life, I had no control.

The Bottom Fell Out

When I was a kid, we often made the short drive to Cedar Point, the nearby amusement park. I always looked forward to one ride: The Rotor! The Rotor was a crazy carnival ride where you climb inside this cylindrical contraption for a true test of your equilibrium—as well as your stomach. They have you stand completely against the inside of cylinder. Slowly it starts spinning and spinning faster and faster, creating intense centrifugal force. This was no ride for the faint of heart or those who cannot handle dizziness and nausea! Now, while you are spinning at a ridiculous speed, they drop the floor down about six feet out from under you! You are then spinning helplessly with no solid footing below, pinned mercilessly against that wall, the ride seemingly endless. You are at the mercy of the ride.

When Sherri was diagnosed with a potentially lethal and rare lymphoma, I found myself drifting mentally, and I was back on The Rotor, spinning helplessly and pinned—or more like plastered—against that wall, with the floor dropped so low I could not see it. The only other person on that ride with me was Sherri. No operator was sitting above watching us, ready to slow us down and bring us back to a stable, grounded world. Stop! Please! I want to get off!

The Background

Many years have passed since the last time I stepped into The Rotor to be willingly spun out of control. Like many young people, sports called to me at a young age. The call led me to an entire career centered around competitive sports. The fierce competitiveness of the game of football had me hooked from the first hit.

When the last seconds ticked off the clock my senior year in high school, little did I know that my deep passion for the game would take me down a specific career path into education so I could teach and coach. Football, they say, is like life. It is not a cliché; the lessons learned in football or other sports are indeed invaluable. There are lessons in athletics that really are unique and can definitely prepare those willing to learn them for life's challenges. For all of these reasons, football defined who I was most of my life—first as a player and then as a high school coach and teacher. When I hung up my whistle, I had no idea that the skills developed as a coach and teacher would be put to a wholly different use when Sherri was diagnosed.

Your Health Is Everything

Until Sherri's diagnosis, I had never really faced any major illness with myself or my family. Sherri has always been extremely healthy. Both our families have long life bloodlines. None of that mattered on that fateful day. It was a day of infamy for our family when Sherri was diagnosed with lymphoma.

This entire book could be about Sherri and cancer, right? Her story as a patient and survivor was the greatest challenge of our lives and is indeed both frightening and incredible at the same time. But there is another story to tell. You see, I became a caregiver in the blink of an eye. And my story is a critical one that often is not told. For every cancer diagnosis, there is a patient. And, you would hope that, for every diagnosed patient, there is someone or some people who will be there to care for them, to help and support them as they wage a battle for their very lives. Sadly, this is not always true as many are all alone in their fight. This would not be the case for my wife—not on my watch. Life prepares you, right? In my case, almost all my life experiences, coupled with a boundless love, enabled me to become a strong and effective caregiver.

What Cancer Does to a Family, a Home

My story, which constitutes half of this book, is to shed light on how cancer, or any life-threatening illness, can impact the family and caregivers. Cancer, in and of itself, thankfully has some powerful enemies out there in the form of science and medicine. This is about how we, the loved ones, react, take action, and completely adjust our daily lives and function on a whole other plane of existence that most are oblivious to. The chances are likely that many, or even most, will be handed the title of caregiver at some stage in life. By sharing my perspectives, emotions, reactions, and actions throughout Sherri's stages of cancer and recovery, you'll discover what you may feel and experience is normal—and it's okay!

What I Observed

The coughing—the relentless coughing. When Sherri started to cough, it didn't take long for it to magnify it into more than just a cough. Sleeping became a serious challenge for both of us. She would lie down and start making a sound like clearing her throat. Then a cough or two. Within minutes, sometimes seconds, she would be sitting up and violently hacking. At times, it was downright unnerving, and I had my phone at the ready to call 911, truly worried that she might stop breathing. The coughing fits reminded me of when you accidentally aspirate a drink or even your own saliva, and the coughing never stops. Literally, there was nothing I could do to help her. I half expected her eyes to blow blood vessels. Frightening. And this went on for weeks, even months. She would come home and tell me about coughing attacks at school.

When she finally had enough, she decided to go to the doctor. This is when the crapshoot began. At first, they thought it might be pneumonia. Oh wait, no, it's bronchitis. Then it was pneumonia on top of bronchitis! It took about three weeks and a couple rounds of different drugs before they finally got serious and took pictures of her chest and lungs. Meanwhile, the coughing went on. Taking prescribed medications and not getting better was getting old in a hurry. We wanted answers, and we wanted them *now*!

Answers We Did Not Want to Hear

Now came quicker than expected. Now turned out to be not so great. When Sherri got the call giving her the preliminary results from a chest x-ray, we were sitting in the car outside a bakery, about to go in for a treat. What do you do when you see the color drain from your soul mate's face and her expression morph from worry to outright fear? The world stopped turning at that moment. I knew then and there the news she was getting was awful. I think Sherri heard only two words in that conversation with the doctor: "nodules" and "cancer." What do you do? What do you say to that sort of news? Man, I sure could have used some guidance. I went to embrace her, and she said she just wanted to go home.

Life Prepares You, Right?

When the CT scan results came back, Sherri called me at school while I was in class. There was silence and then sobbing. She was distraught. She proceeded to tell me that the doctor told her it really appeared to be lung cancer. *Cancer?* Whoa. I was unprepared for that. I have a classroom full of sophomore US History students just inside the door. I know they must be wondering what is going on because this is completely out of routine— though it soon would be normal for me to step out of my classroom to take a phone call.

I had to shift into damage control and an immediate "calm-her-down" mode. I needed to get Sherri back to a point where I could talk to her and she could respond coherently. I have two battles going on here. Trying to get the details from Sherri and ease her anxiety while at the same time eyeball the classroom and try to make the call as short as possible so I was not derelict in my duties. Yes, that was just a prelude of what was to come next in my life.

In that moment, the school and classroom melted away, and all that really mattered was Sherri. There are times for words of solace and comfort, and there are times for no words at all. I just let her vent and cry before speaking.

13

Once able to talk more calmly, she filled me in that they were referring her to a cardiothoracic surgeon at the James Cancer Hospital at the Ohio State University Wexner Medical Center. Things were getting real. As the conversation finally came to an end, I could tell a new emotion was arising in Sherri: anger. The fighter was emerging. My challenge, although I was unaware of it yet, would be to feed the fighter and starve the fear.

Is She Sick or Not?

Something that threw me for a loop more than once was this unforeseen roller-coaster ride prior to diagnosis. One day, Sherri was coughing her lungs right out of her chest. The next, she was just fine and feeling well. That four-month window of hell before the doctors finally nailed down the lymphoma was filled with these on-and-off stretches of calm and seemingly good health for Sherri.

The good days were a façade. Truthfully, it was a time of high anxiety with some calm peppered in. We squeezed in some good times, some concerts, and a spring break trip, leading us to believe she was OK, but in reality, we were just biding our time and waiting for the bottom to fall out—just like The Rotor. If I could go back and handle that time differently, I am certain I would have had more direct conversations with the physicians and surgeon to push for more definitive answers. Easy to say now of course, hindsight being twenty-twenty.

An Unwanted "Promotion" in Rank

We had a brief respite when a biopsy with a specialist showed what was believed to be a fungal infection and not cancer, and some antifungal meds were prescribed.

Weeks later, when the cardiothoracic surgeon called to check in and suggest a scan just to be certain Sherri was in the clear, we had no idea how life was about to change. This phone call, which inevitably saved her life, would throw Sherri into the maelstrom of a medical nightmare and turn our normal lives upside down. You must understand that he had no reason to call. Since lung cancer was ruled out, Sherri was no longer in his care; he was not her primary care physician. This man called out of pure concern to make sure she was actually doing as well clinically as she seemed to be feeling. He is a saint in my book.

The diagnosis that followed another scan and biopsy would change our lives forever. As a football coach, I always preached the following anecdotes to my teams:

1. Expect the unexpected. Though you cannot predict them, unexpected events are coming your way throughout life.
2. Hope for the best—but prepare for the worst.

I was about the get schooled on what these truly meant.

The moment the diagnosis was handed down, I received a "promotion" I had no desire to receive. The rank of "caregiver" was given to me, without any pomp and circumstance—and within the context of a five-minute phone call. The surgeon called us on my phone late in the morning on that fateful day. Wisely, I did not put the call on speaker, but I took careful notes. He explained to me that the results were in. Sherri's body was under attack, and the invader was a fast-growing, vicious enemy. Cancer. Time was of the essence. I remained calm through the call: Sherri was watching me intently, like a hawk. I remember glancing at her and thinking, *Oh my God. I have to hang up in just seconds and tell my wife she actually does have cancer after all. So much for a fungal infection.*

My duties were thrust upon me in the blink of an eye. Having canceled a celebratory family trip after the biopsy now seemed prophetic. We were not going anywhere. A plethora of questions were going through my head. WTF? How did this happen? What are we going to do? How is she going to survive this? How am I going to get her through this? Wait! Calm down! The doctor is still talking, and I need to listen.

He was making a referral directly to the oncology department at the James and said that they would be reaching out to us to schedule Sherri and assign her to her to an oncologist. We would need to wait for the call. Now the questions became a tidal wave rolling through my mind: Wait, what about the fungal infection you guys said was all she had? We have to *wait* for them to call us? Is this curable? Most importantly, could I lose her? My head spun. It was beyond emotional. We were raw and frightened out of our minds. Literally, within an hour or two, we got a call from the James. Sherri was assigned and scheduled to see the oncologist in exactly one week. That was one long week.

The moment the diagnosis was given, my mind started racing, thinking about our current medical insurance, hospital care, life insurance (God forbid), and even worse things like what if she isn't going to come out of this. Congratulations, John Snoad. You are now elevated and commissioned to the high rank of caregiver! Good luck! While I would welcome luck, I was not going to wait for it. No way! I decided almost instantly that I was going get control of this situation, and fast.

Takeaways

- ✦ Life can change in a heartbeat. I know it is cliché, but I am a believer now.
- ✦ Expect the unexpected. Prepare for the worst and hope for the best is easy to say, but I wasn't walking around every day wondering when a calamity would hit. However, my advice is to always make sure your "medical ducks" are in a row.
  - o Make sure you know your health insurance coverage.
  - o Have a plan if there is an emergency and who you will turn to.
  - o It may be an uncomfortable topic, but at least have some sort of simple will.
  - o Life insurance? Thank God it was not a factor here, but what if it had been? Having some small policy ensures you can take care of a funeral if need be. Again, I know this is morbid, but it has to be considered.
  - o Even consider something as simple as travel insurance. With the sudden cancelation of our trip to Europe, I was able to get all monies refunded. That money came in handy later.
- ✦ Deal with it aggressively, face it head-on, and be the sort of caregiver who eases worry and removes responsibility from the patient, allowing them to use their energies for fighting the disease. I made the decision to not settle for anything less than the best care, and when I wanted answers, I never let up until I got them. I have no regrets and highly recommend this approach.
- ✦ Be strong, be steady, and be the rock your loved one needs. Your needs are secondary now. Your focus must become one that is entirely supportive.

CHAPTER 2A: SHERRI

Summer of Chemo

Holding Onto What I Could

Once again worry, wait, worry, and wait some more. Sitting in the waiting room to see the oncologist, my first of many times, I noticed blank faces around me, everyone nodding subdued pleasantries, while feeling the weight, fear, and dread for our own conditions. The sadness in the fairly large lobby-like waiting area was like a dark and ominous cloud just hanging there above our heads. John and I didn't say much, both of us feeling anxious and wondering what would come next.

Scans, Pokes, and Tests

My turn came. I was called back to face the reality of what was going on. Along with drawing several vials of blood came all the standard questions: Was I feeling OK? Did I have an appetite? Had I lost weight? Had I fallen recently? Did I feel fatigued? OK, get on with it. I was numb to all of this by now. Let's get to the appointment and get answers! The only thing keeping me from screaming, "Let me off of this ride!" was the kindness of the staff, my wonderful oncologist, and his nurse practitioner, who I came to look forward to seeing.

The oncologist and nurse practitioner were both calm and reassuring. I was listening and nodding to everything they said, but the words didn't register. I was starring as a patient in this show, not the supporting role of nurse as I was used to being. Big plot twist: it was my life on the line, and all I kept hearing was "cancer" and lymphoma." The rest drifted right over my head. There was just one question I really wanted the answer to, and it was a doozy. You have those moments in life when you really want to know something—or you really don't want to know because the answer may not be what you want to hear.

I finally asked the one big question: "Is this treatable?" I had been afraid to ask if it was a death sentence. I will always remember the oncologist's answer. Without missing a beat and full of confidence, the oncologist said "Yes, it's not only treatable; it's curable." Tears flowed, and relief and hope flooded over me. I had some control and could fight. Those words often served as beacons of hope at my lowest points. I would draw strength from those words.

The next week was a whirlwind filled with more scans, blood draws, and lumbar punctures. Over the course of my treatments, I endured five lumbar punctures, commonly known as a spinal tap, each one causing horrendous headaches. These headaches can last for days, and I ended up in the emergency room twice due to the agony they caused.

All these new scans, pokes, prods, and tests were just to get ready for chemotherapy. My God, what was the actual treatment going to be like? The plan was to receive six full rounds of chemotherapy in total, and each round would require inpatient stay from Monday through Friday. I would be receiving five intravenous bags in total, and each one would go in over twenty-four hours. They called it the "cocktail." A cocktail, isn't that cute? I would much rather have a strawberry daiquiri or a mojito. I had never seen that mixture on a cocktail menu—and I hope to never see it anywhere again. No matter what chemo was called, the only thing I cared about was that it would work.

Let's Get It Started

Walking into the hospital to be admitted that first time is not a clear memory, but I do remember thinking my life as I knew it was over, and this new life was spinning out of control. Realizing I needed to fight and giving up wasn't an option, my mental attitude needed to be tough. It needed to be positive. There was no negotiating this; the stakes were too high. I took inventory of what I could control and focused on those things every day.

We Can Fix That. Here, Take This.

Once I was completely in the hands of science and medicine, it seemed like everything was out of my control and in the hands of my medical team. The medical team plugged IV bags into me, and they decided what was going in, how much, and when. They told me when to show up, when to go home, and everything in between.

In this modern and ever-expanding world of social media, "There's an app for that" has become a common phrase. At the hospital, they have their own version of that little saying: "There's a drug for that."

The side effects from my chemotherapy varied from day to day. To stay on top of it and manage symptoms, the hospital staff was always asking me a barrage of questions: Was I experiencing nausea, dizziness, headaches, or fevers? If I complained about any side effects at all, they had the solution "Here, take this." A pill was kindly given to me. If they said take it, I took it, especially early on.

Wait, isn't anyone worried about the side effects of taking these additional meds? Looking back now and thinking about all the science flowing through my veins is astounding. In the beginning, I wanted to be the model patient. It would not be until later in treatment that I began to ask questions and make decisions for myself relative to taking these additional meds. Getting involved with my care helped me regain some of the control and self-confidence.

No Gowns for This Girl

I had lost control of my life. Period. And yet, there were things that could be controlled—with the most important being attitude. If life is 1 percent what happens to you and 99 percent how you react, that means I could control a lot! For starters, I was *not* going to lay in a hospital gown, bedridden and looking like a dying cancer patient. No way was that going to define me! So, instead of wearing a hospital gown, you could always find me in a running shirt and yoga pants. This empowered me mentally because it identified me as a person, not a patient. I like to believe that the medical team seeing me in my "battle attire," would recognize me as someone who was strong and willing to do all it would take to beat that disease. If I were giving it my all, they would give it their all to cure me!

Move!

Walking and movement were totally in my control. I walked and walked; my IV pole and I were forced to become best friends. Her name was "Ivy," and we went everywhere together. The James is a standalone twenty-one story building, and each floor was a loop. Meeting my daily lap quota became a personal cause: the rule was if you did four laps a day, you did not have to get heparin (an anticoagulant) shots to prevent blood clots from inactivity. If they told me to do four, I did eight or even more! John would take Ivy and me on dates. We would walk the floor, and then we ventured to other floors and even the lobby for a change of scenery. All the floors looked the same. It was just the thrill and slight adrenaline rush of sneaking off my floor, like a kid missing curfew to stay at the party a little bit longer.

We even received permission to venture outside where we would walk around campus. We weren't really supposed to go that far away from the building, just out on the lawn, in case Ivy's alarms started beeping, but I knew how to silence her and which buttons to press to make her happy again—so out on the campus we went. Such rebels!

We sat on benches overlooking a small lake or watched people walking around campus. The walks kept my sanity at a manageable level and my mind in a better place than if I had just sat there wasting away in that hospital room. Holding on to something that I as a person, not the cancer girl, loved to do was crucial. For me, staying physically active mattered. However, this did start to diminish as the treatments started to take their toll on my body and lungs. It became increasingly difficult to muster up the energy. Losing the ability to be active was worrisome and scared me.

Dinner is Served

During hospital stays, the exciting rendezvouses John planned gave me something to anticipate. They were often "dinner" dates. John would take me on a special date to the cafeteria or have food delivered from a restaurant. Movie nights involved popcorn and streaming a movie. These little surprises were a real mental pick-me-up that kept my mind where it needed to be so I could keep fighting.

The Higher Power

Faith is a powerful component for fighting and healing from disease. I prayed regularly to my higher power. A friend gave me a glass charm with a mustard seed in it and a quote from Jesus: "If you have the faith of a mustard seed, nothing shall be impossible" (Matthew 17:20 New Jerusalem Bible).

Trying to maintain faith was difficult somedays, but being in touch with my higher power allowed me to delve more deeply into myself and find strength I didn't know I had—but knew I needed. There were always signs along the way that brought me peace when I was down. God was with me, offering his love and support, whether it be a rainbow outside my window when I was experiencing a bad day, a kind word, or much needed good news from a doctor.

There often were signs that brought me hope if I was open to seeing them. Lying in a hospital bed on my fiftieth birthday, not in a good place mentally, a woman came to my room to deliver balloons. She was working at the information desk in the lobby of that huge hospital. She told me she didn't know why, but she felt compelled to bring the balloons to me.

As we chatted, she shared that on her fiftieth birthday, she was also fighting cancer in the hospital. We went on to talk for more than twenty minutes about how we both had three boys and that we both had one son followed by twins. I will never know her name or remember what she looked like, but I will forever remember her and how our conversation lifted me out of a dark place. I always chose to see those special moments as signs from above.

Lessons Learned

1. While we can't predict the outcome of something like cancer, we can certainly control how we react to it and how we fight it. Maintain who you are. Do not allow the disease to define you. Instead, accept that it is just something that is happening or has happened to you. It is not you.

2. Your attitude of hope elevates your power despite the illness attempting to defeat you. Hope is being able to see that glimmer of light, however dim, at the end of the tunnel.

3. An attitude of hope is as much a part of fighting the disease and healing as the science they may be pumping into your body.

4. Open your eyes and heart to the little things. Your higher power, whomever or whatever that means to you, may be sending signs of hope. Embrace and hold onto the blessings and little things that come along as you battle through this. Some days, that may be all you have to get through the day.

CHAPTER 2B: JOHN

The Juggling Act Begins

Don't Lose Your Balance!

At least now we know what the hell is wrong. But how on earth are they, and we, going to fight this?

The surgeon emphasized that this lymphoma was rare, and that was one reason they kept missing the mark. None of that mattered now. I had a mission to perform, and it was a difficult one at that. The organizer, the doer, and the planner in me came to life.

Once we had that initial appointment, even though we had no real concept for the treatment protocol to come, I pulled out my calendar and started plotting. I had no choice due to the immediacy of things. I was entering another year of coaching high school football, and we were already into our summer workout regimen. Instruction and full-day practices were on the horizon. Initially, I believed that caregiving would be doable, and I would be able to manage my professional responsibilities as a coach and teacher once school started while balancing being a caregiver. No two ways about it, I would manage things and manage them well. Sometimes the best-laid plans simply don't work out.

We had to wait a full seven days until the initial meeting with oncology. However, my first obstacle popped up almost immediately: Sherri. I am married to someone with two key characteristics that together made for some real dicey situations, starting with the diagnosis. Sherri is stubborn and headstrong as a rule. When she decides something, consider it decided and just get out of the way. She is also a nurse. In fact, she did home health care and hospice as part of her nursing career. Put those two things together, and you have the recipe for a caregiver's nightmare.

Sherri began doggedly researching her lymphoma. Intervention was necessary immediately before she researched herself into an emotional frenzy and permanent state of panic. I had done enough research already to know that this truly was a rare lymphoma, they did not know all that much about it, and survival was a fifty-fifty chance. This could take her life.

As soon as I read some of these details, it was imperative that I convince Sherri to stay off the web! "Dr. Google" is an extremely dangerous resource and can be terribly misleading. My God, if she started reading this stuff, her emotional well-being would be in the sewer. It would put her in a dark place of worry and paranoia that she might not be able to come out of. Did she listen? At first, no. I caught her a few times and literally had to close the laptop on her. She read enough to start the panic ball rolling, and it started to snowball. Finally, after one occasion of reading what it could do to her, she threw her hands up and surrendered, vowing to not read or research anymore. One obstacle cleared.

Secretary or Psychologist?

The first appointment taught me instantly that one of my primary caregiving roles was going to be "Mr. Secretary." Sherri will bluntly tell you that she ceased being a nurse when the diagnosis was made, and in that moment, she became a patient. At this first appointment with the oncologist, and literally all the appointments thereafter, including visits to her hospital room when in treatment, I discovered that I needed to step up, take seriously thorough notes, track dates, and log incidents and changes. I needed to get familiar with all the medical lingo, write down the gigantic words, spell them correctly (so I could look them up later), and be able to explain it all to Sherri, our sons, family, and friends. Most of all, I needed to be able to explain what the doctor said to Sherri. She would not hear the full conversation or big picture of what was said. She could only pull out key words or phrases, which then became her reality. Caregivers are the ears, eyes, and often voices for the patient.

Sherri often wasn't hearing anything clearly or correctly. We would leave the doctor on numerous occasions with me feeling confident about the plan or prognosis they had for her. As soon as we would get to the car, I would get this look of doom from her and statements about her "pending death." She was clearly panicked. She would look at me and ask, "Am I going to die? I am not going to make it, am I?"

The first couple of times, I would cock my head, look at her, and wonder if she was at the same appointment I had been at. I would say, "Uh, no, that is not what was said at all!"

Eventually, I knew this was coming and would smile or chuckle in anticipation of her remarks, which, led to my other major role: the patient whisperer. I was the guy who had to repeatedly talk her off the edge of the cliff. If you are, or will be, a caregiver, plan on having to do this often. I literally would have to walk her through all my notes and take her step-by-step through the appointment to reassure her they had a plan, they knew what they were doing, and it was going to work.

By then, Sherri getting stuck with needles was a regular occurrence. At the first appointment, and at every oncology appointment thereafter, step 1 was check in, step 2 was waiting in the lobby, and step 3 was getting called back where the nurses would draw her blood. Then it was back to an exam room.

I took a ton of notes, but I vividly remember one thing: the oncologist telling Sherri she would be *cured*. Yes, cured! She had asked if her lymphoma was treatable, and he unequivocally said it was not only treatable—but curable. She lit up as bright as the sun and burst into tears. Little did we know the price that would have to be paid for that cure.

The focus of that first appointment turned toward the science of her treatment plan. She was going to be admitted in a week's time after another of series of tests, probes, and pokes. I knew what my role was instantly: hold her hand, comfort her, and be her advocate. I was husband, caregiver, cheerleader, secretary, coach, advocate, and champion hugger.

Sherri's trip on a road through hell, the one to get her life back, began early on a Monday morning in June. We reported to the James, and she was to be admitted for five days and four nights. Did we just win a trip to a twenty-one-story resort hotel?

Cue the Game Show Announcer

"Well, Sherri, I say, yes, you, Sherri Snoad, will be admitted into the luxurious studio-like rooms of the beautiful and new James Cancer Hospital and Solove Research Institute for four glorious nights! You will enjoy our full, round-the-clock service, meals prepared especially for you, views of breathtaking downtown Columbus, Ohio, and the campus of *the* Ohio State University, a flat-screen TV with complimentary movies, and, wait for it, on top of all that, your own personal, 'knock you off your feet' cocktail fed intravenously into your arm! Luxury awaits you!"

OK, so I exaggerated a bit. The James at the Ohio State University is a beautiful facility and a far cry from the dingy old hospital rooms that we all have seen. High ceilings, light colors, and gigantic floor-to-ceiling windows truly made the patient feel like they were not being held in a cell waiting for death. When they sent us to our room on the sixteenth floor, I immediately jumped into my role. I helped her unpack her things, set her rolling tray up with necessities, and just made her comfortable. She was quite nervous about it, and I tried to keep things light and assure her that I was not going anywhere. This began a series of many long stays in the hospital. I vowed she would never spend a night alone. I slept on a pullout couch in her room each night.

The mind can certainly wreak havoc, can't it? When they came in and began prepping Sherri for the "hookup" to her IV, they walked us through the chemo cocktail regimen she would be receiving. The one thing the oncologist reiterated to us was this: Sherri's type of lymphoma was a fast-growing cancer. Potency was particularly important with the drugs. They said that fast-growing cells are the ones that would be impacted first. This was a good thing, right? Indeed, it was.

Any fast-growing cells in the body would be killed off first. This meant the lymphoma would be under full assault right away. I used these words to reassure Sherri that this was great news, and the doctor also said that we should start to see results after the first few treatments. I was ecstatic, and Sherri did find some comfort in this. Throughout all of this, I continuously reminded myself to record everything said and reassure Sherri that we had heard the doctors correctly. She was going to beat this!

The Rounds Begin!

Once the IV pump began, I found myself going on high alert. Like I said, the mind can do funny things, even to a caregiver. I was expecting the worst in terms of side effects. I pictured Sherri bent over puking, swooning, and on the verge of passing out. Anytime the IV pump alarm sounded on the pole she wheeled around, I panicked inside. It did not help that at first, the chemotherapy went into an IV in her arm. Every few minutes, she would forget and bend her arm and "beep-beep-beep!" Good God, let it end! Every time that damn thing went off, we had to buzz the nurse. Thankfully, they surgically installed a "power port" up high on her chest, eliminating the problem.

Round 1 came and went. Sherri made it through like a champ! And so, this began what I like to call the vicious circle. Twenty-one days became our new "month." She would be admitted on day 1 of the cycle, receive her five straight days of twenty-four-hour, round-the-clock chemical drips, get discharged on day 5, and then have a sixteen-day recovery window. Ups and downs? Too many to recount during that sixteen-day window, but by the end of each, she would generally be back to a place where her body could handle another round.

I didn't see much change in her during that first cycle. I was looking for her to either start losing weight or to be gaining it from bloating. Hell, I thought her hair would fall out during the first round. Apparently, hair follicles are considered fast-growing cell producers, so we knew it was coming. They said all fast-growing cells are impacted first. Her hair was as full and thick as ever, and it would not start falling out until after round 2. Rounds 2 and 3 followed, and for the most part, it all went smoothy. The oncologist predicted her chemo would be finished by October, and a return to normalcy would soon follow. Sometimes the best laid plans fail.

Balancing Act

Though school was not in session yet, I was at football practice and planning meetings full-time by Sherri's second round. Thank goodness I wasn't yet having to do daily teaching plans yet and teach six classes all day. There was much to do—managing the house and finances, yard upkeep, the pets, the mail, cleaning—but all that was secondary in nature to what really mattered. Though challenging to manage at times, I spent every night at the hospital with Sherri, only stopping in at home for fresh clothes and to check up on things. Oftentimes, I would wake up at the hospital, drive to football, and then come right back—or stop at home first and then head to the hospital. I was only a call away if they said I needed to be there. I was emphatic when I assured her I would handle everything at home. She just needed to focus all her energies on fighting this monster. I needed to focus all mine on making sure she had nothing to distract her.

Getting Your Shit Together

Caregivers must have their shit together. Period. One cannot just wing it. I had to account for all the intangibles and unexpected problems and keep accurate records of everything related to Sherri and the hospital and the myriad medical personnel we were encountering. I needed to document all discussions, consultations, and plans.

Luckily at home, since I manage the finances, it was just a matter of making sure I was careful to avoid mistakes and not rush through paying bills and making insurance payments and house payments. Some sage advice: get away from your loved one when handling issues and controversies in your financial life or even when updating family on her condition (she did not need to hear me rambling about things that were going on).

I knew enough to know that Sherri was under enough duress, and she did not need to hear me on the phone with insurance companies, banks, credit card companies, employers, or anyone else I may have to contend with about a bill, a dispute, sick time, whatever. I found myself often doing recordkeeping, paying bills, and handling problems after she fell asleep, both at home and when we were at the hospital. If I had to be on the phone when she was awake, I went to the lounge, an empty hospital room, down to the basement, or out on the back porch—anywhere that was out of earshot. It became important to use all my time away from Sherri to handle these stress-inducing situations.

I hate being in the car. We have always lived close to work to avoid long drives in rush hour traffic. I seemed to be in the car a lot more during those days. I was juggling time in the triangular pattern of school, football (I was coaching across town at a different school from where I taught), and back to the hospital or home. I came to relish those times in the car because it provided some "me" time to mentally unwind or prepare myself and plan for what might lay ahead.

At the hospital, my time was for Sherri. As she got further into the treatment, she started to sleep more and more frequently, both in the hospital and at home. I utilized those moments to handle business, do yard work, prep for class, and do whatever else needed to be done. I am fairly good at multitasking, and those skills were put to the test every day.

I was pretty darn successful at shielding Sherri from all this. To this day, I wonder how on earth someone could possibly go through this illness alone. And when it would get really hard, and she was facing the unforeseen complications, I would wonder how anyone could do that alone. It boggles the mind to no end to consider how difficult that would be.

Trusting the Pros

Throughout that summer of chemo, I watched science and the oncology team take over Sherri's body. Despite my concerns, both Sherri and I had to turn this over to the professionals. We had to trust these men and women charged with her care—implicitly. Most of the doctors were amazingly transparent. A few, not so much. The doctors who were not forthright were the ones who had a lot of questions to answer. I would not let them leave the room until we knew everything. We had a great team who we trusted, and we let them do their thing. Her team had one mission: kill the cancer and make Sherri a member of the statistical group known as "survivors." They were committed to making that happen. Knowing how rare and aggressive this lymphoma was, we were truly fortunate to have a team of OSU's most experienced physicians and staff fighting for her life. We trusted that we were in good hands.

Eye-Opening Lifestyle Changes

Based upon years of treating patients and doing research studies and trials, they really presented us with a well-rounded treatment plan. This included dietary education and planning. I soon discovered that I was now going to become a dietitian of sorts. When we were not at the hospital, Sherri would have to be protected from bacteria, germs, viruses, and anything else that could expose her to sickness.

A by-product of killing the cancer was the annihilation of her immune system. Being immunocompromised meant Sherri became entirely susceptible to colds, flu, bronchitis, and pneumonia, which could be deadly to anyone who was immunocompromised. Consequently, it was made clear to me that her diet, though not terribly restrictive, would be subject to foods she could stomach and that were carefully cleaned and meticulously prepared.

If we were going to have a salad, the vegetables and lettuce had to be thoroughly cleaned and scrubbed. They told me to rinse veggies under running water for twenty seconds. Doesn't sound too bad, right? Try it. Put the book down, go get a pepper or an apple out of the fridge, and rinse that thing for twenty seconds. It's an eternity! I was shocked at how little we really were cleaning our foods before we ate or prepared them. Who washes an orange before peeling it? Well, think about it. The peel is coated with dirt, germs, and chemicals. The second you dig into it, you get that stuff on your fingers and under your nails, and you drive the germs right into the fruit. Even with canned goods, did you ever stop to think what germs were living on that lid before you popped the seal with the can opener and cranked it around, sending all that crud right into the can? This was eye-opening! So, you can bet I became a champion food cleaner and preparer.

This Is No Fad Diet. It Is a Life Change.

We had to eat a variety of healthy, high-fiber foods and cut down on fats and sugars. Luckily, this wasn't a hard transition since we typically ate healthy, having made some permanent changes to our diets the previous year. This is where caregiver duties become really critical. An unforeseen challenge was how to deal with all the well-meaning friends who showed up at our door with salads, pastas, and other easy meals. I had no way of knowing if they took the necessary steps to prepare, and a lot of this food showed up before I could get the word out. If the boys were home, I would let them chow it down. But Sherri? Not a chance. Even ordering out was a bit dicey. I was not willing to risk takeout for a while. I just wasn't ready to trust that the food had been prepared safely enough for someone who was immunocompromised.

Mr. Clean

The house was another big challenge. It had to be meticulously cleaned. During Sherri's first round, on one of my trips home, I cleaned the house from top to bottom, having transformed into the latest version of "Mr. Clean." I know that we live in a world where getting rid of chemicals and using all-natural solutions is a popular and truly awesome trend, but in this case, I couldn't buy enough cleaning agents. Looking back, I now realize that

I should have been more selective, but I went with what I knew and was in overdrive to get it done.

Our house had never been so spick-and-span. And even though we have pets, I deodorized and bathed them. I purchased canisters of bleach wipes and daily sanitized light switches and doorknobs, TV remotes, and anything else Sherri would be frequently touching. The toilets were cleaned daily. This was no fly-by-night operation. Floors were hand scrubbed, carpets shampooed, and sinks scoured. I sprayed down the furniture with deodorizing and germ-killing sprays. As a caregiver, diligence is the name of the game—and you cross every t and dot every i. Hell, even the car had to be cleaned regularly because she had to get into it so often.

When school started, and I was back in the classroom, I noticed every cough and sneeze. At the risk of being rude, I established rules: students had to step into the hall to blow their noses or cough and immediately use the hand sanitizer I provided. Interesting that this became the norm during the COVID-19 pandemic.

I told all my students what was happening with Mrs. Snoad and how I could take no chances. The students were amazingly supportive, and soon they just did what was asked without being reminded. Just being in a classroom and seeing my 170 plus students throughout the day, or passing the hundreds of others in the hallways, clearly there was a high risk of being exposed to germs. I would come home, immediately remove my work clothes, place them in the laundry, and hit the shower to clean off before I kissed Sherri and said hello. What a regimented life we were living!

Germophobia: The Struggle Is Real

Sherri's cancer impacted both of us immensely. To this day, we both are terribly germophobic. Whether at church, a restaurant, a theater, or literally anywhere else, if someone is coughing or sneezing, we move. We hand sanitize all the time, and Sherri avoids opening doors to public places unless she is alone, and even then, she uses her sleeve to cover her hand. When we travel on a plane, we bring bleach wipes. Our seats, trays, seat belts, and arm rests are cleaner than the day they were manufactured! People may look at us curiously, but I think they wish I would clean their seats too! It is now a normal part of our travel routine. An ounce of prevention is worth a pound of cure.

Storm Clouds Looming

Sherri was about to start the fourth round of chemo. Rounds 4 through 6 would follow and then, voila, she would be done, home and recovering so she could get back into life again. Hurray! Hell, yes! Let's get it done! But look out because things are about to take an unexpected turn.

Takeaways

1. You don't know what you don't know. We probably say this half a dozen times in this book, but you really cannot hear this enough: until you are directly involved as either the patient or a caregiver, you really have no idea what people are going through. Both our eyes were opened.
2. Do whatever it takes. What other choice is there? As a caregiver, you'll learn to juggle and balance out of necessity. If you were disorganized before, this situation will set you straight.
3. Listen and learn to do all you can to arm yourself well as caregiver. Read all materials given and become informed—and keep the patient off the internet!
4. Take every precaution. In our case, it was cleaning, sanitizing, and being careful about protecting Sherri's immunocompromised body.
5. Be there—always. Luckily, I was blessed to be able to stay at the hospital and sleep in Sherri's room every step of the way. For others, this may be difficult, especially with little ones at home and/or no family are around to help. Just be there as much as possible. Your loved one needs this—whether they say so or not.

CHAPTER 3A: SHERRI

Time to Get Wiggy with It!

Reality Check

Well, now it's getting real. Before starting chemotherapy, the doctors warned me I would be losing my hair. Having a nursing background and experiences in home health care and hospice many years earlier, I knew it would happen. But with everything else going on during treatment, losing my hair wasn't really something I was worrying about. The reality of the situation was that I was still unsure about what the diagnosis meant and what the treatment would entail. My daily goals were to simply get through the activities of everyday life.

I Knew This Was Coming (Sort Of)

Someone came into my room during the first round of treatment to discuss helping me set up an appointment for a wig fitting, which I agreed to. *OK, whatever, no big deal. I'll go along with it.*

Though clearly informed that my hair would indeed fall out, I didn't really grasp the fact that I would actually lose ALL of my hair. Just in case the doctor was correct, I spoke to my hairdresser and if—but it probably won't happen to me (yeah right)—the time came, she said she would shave my hair off.

Sometime after round 2, here and there, I began to notice some hair on my pillow or in my hand while taking a shower. Other than thinking it was just a little bit of shedding, I didn't give it much thought. Then it hit. It just happened. While resting on our back porch and mindlessly running fingers through my hair, a huge clump came out. I was *terrified!* This was different from the fear I felt at the time of the diagnosis. This was like a big smack in the head. *OK, girl you can't deny this, you've got cancer!* Yes, it was a reality check like no other.

Showing John the big clump of hair I was holding, I cried, "Shave my head—right now!"

He was a master at using his hair clippers to give our boys buzz cuts when they were young. I never imagined he would be using them on me. There is no recollection of what was said—just the gentleness of him sitting me in a chair and shaving my head while we both had tears running down our cheeks. This is a memory that I hold deep in my heart. My tears turned into sobs. The emotion welled up and just came pouring out.

You may be thinking that's pretty vain for me to be so worried about my hair, but the actual physical part of losing my hair wasn't what I was crying about. The tears were about the reality of it. *I have cancer! This is for real.*

From that day on, John would rub my head every day and tell me how beautiful I was, and I could see in his eyes that he really meant it. Even though I didn't feel very pretty, he always made me feel special.

The Fitting

Getting a wig was not an experience to look forward to. Though hopeful a wig would disguise the feeling that I was losing myself along with my hair, and that no one would notice, it turned out to be wishful thinking. Since I had already lost my hair, it was important to bring along some photos of what I looked like with hair for the stylist to see.

The wig stylist really was amazing, and she spent so much time with me. She was energetic and playful, and she was also compassionate. In the end, I decided to go with two wigs that were both similar to my hairstyle, but they gave some options, depending on my mood. There was the proper, every hair in place wig, but when I was feeling like a badass, it was the wilder, spiked hair wig for me!

I Hate This Thing

Sadly, it did not take long for me to dread putting on my wig. They were so hot and smothering. Never take a nap in a wig! I did once and woke up with it over my eyes. Good advice is to remember that wigs and naps do not work in harmony with each other. They seemed to have a mind of their own. At first, I donned them often, but as chemo decimated my body and strength, being bald didn't matter much anymore. No wig could disguise what my mind and body were experiencing.

Some friends got me scarves to wear and style around my head. It was such a kind gesture, but I just wasn't into it. Eventually, a simple baseball cap did the trick and became my standard headwear. The cap felt more like me and was quite comfortable. There was an upside to being bald: it was great when getting ready to go somewhere. Now it was me, not John, who was always the first one ready when we would go somewhere. I never had to worry about bad hair days. How is that for making a positive out of a negative?

Losing my hair was traumatic, but the baldness wasn't the most horrible thing that could happen. I looked at the positives. Losing the hair meant I wasn't waiting to die; it meant I was getting treatment and attacking the cancer head-on!

Look Good, Feel Good!

A program offered by the American Cancer Society called "Look Good, Feel Good" was suggested to me by a friend. Taking a deep breath, I walked into a room full of women who were each sporting wig or scarf, exchanging pleasantries, and acting as if this was just your average night out with friends. In truth, we were all faking it; everyone there was unsure of what to expect. Initially, there was an apprehensive energy; after all, we were there for the same reason. Everyone there may have been at different stages or facing different types, but we all had cancer, so our interactions with each other were defined by this and not by who we were individually.

At the "Look Good, Feel Good" program, we were treated as beautiful women who deserved to be pampered and feel feminine. The atmosphere of this "girl's night out" though, was a bit tense as everyone was apprehensive to reveal their inner, scarred selves. That is, until one woman said, "It's hot in here! I can't stand this wig anymore!" So, whoosh! In one swift pull, off it came, baring her beautiful bald head.

There was a collective sigh and then a host of laughs as the rest of us wearing wigs did the same thing. That one person was following the "you do you" motto, and in doing so, she gave all of us the courage to just "do you" too.

For the rest of the evening, we learned to use and apply makeup in ways that would help address issues often experienced while undergoing treatment. Everyone received a bag of makeup and skin care products from some of the top names in the industry! Walking away that evening not feeling alone anymore, I realized that cancer is not picky—and I had not been singled out for any particular reason. Age, wealth, status, skin color, and religion simply do not matter. Cancer does not discriminate. Cancer doesn't give a damn who you are. This one single word, *cancer*, forever binds together those of us who have been, or are, afflicted with it in a way no one else can really understand.

Survivor Programs

After the "Look Good, Feel Good" experience, I wanted more opportunities to connect with others like me. I explored some of the survivorship programs available through the hospital where I received treatment and researched offerings through community agencies as well. John came along and was my personal chauffeur since I was restricted from driving. He enjoyed going because there were other caregivers who had the same struggles and concerns he did. These activities provided fun little ways to escape even for just an hour or two and not sit at home thinking about all that was going on.

The wonderful thing is that most communities have many offerings that are free for cancer patients, survivors, and caregivers. I had no idea the extent of this whole other world until I became ill, and even then I had no realization for the vast services that are out there. When searching your area, look at hospital-based, community-based, and national organizations that offer classes or can direct you to helpful resources. For me, these activities and programs were a real outlet and a great way to help us cope. John and I got to meet and talk to so many others who were on this same journey, sharing stories and getting tips on how to handle this or that.

Much of the time, we did not know where this cancer journey was going. With just a little support, we didn't have to fumble our way through the cancer world entirely blindfolded; it was more like dark sunglasses. When people I know have told me they are battling cancer, I always make sure to recommend getting involved in programs being offered and looking beyond the hospital programs to the many support organizations available.

Lessons Learned

1. Finding the good in something that's not so good. OK, this is going to sound strange, but looking back, I can honestly say I liked having the opportunity of living without hair. I learned much from the experience. The hair loss was devastating in the moment but realizing you don't need hair to look and feel beautiful is beautiful in itself.

2. You are still you. Hair or no hair, I'm still me—and I still love everything about life. At first, the belief that it's necessary to fit the stereotypical cancer patient who loses hair and needs a wig may feel strong. I thought I was supposed to feel that way. I hated that wig. Why do we need to hide behind a mask? Everyone who knows us will know it's a wig anyway.

3. You do you. Wear a wig or don't. Wear makeup or don't. Walking around bald as a woman spurs people to use the pity card on you. So, what! That is their problem, not yours. Shine your bald head with pride. Use it to your advantage if you like! If they want to move you to the front of the line or give you a seat when everyone is standing and waiting for a table at a restaurant, how cool is that? Might as well take advantage!

4. You will be different. Embrace it! A few months after chemo, my hair grew back with a fun surprise: curls! Chemo curls! My hair had always been straight, unless you count the perms of the 1980s, which I think we all want to forget. At first, I didn't know what to think of them, and every time someone would compliment me on my curls, I felt the need to explain they were the result of chemotherapy. "Oh, those are my chemo curls," I would say. Of course, that brought on pity and a rehashing of all I had gone through. Finally, there came a time I just smiled and said thanks when I got compliments on my curls! After a few years though my curls went away. I was bummed and had to adjust once again to something taken away that was out of my control.

5. Acceptance. Self-pity is natural when life presents us with obstacles. I spent too much time trying to figure out why that happened to me and what I had done to deserve it. What a waste of my precious

time. Wallowing in self-pity, coupled with fear and worry, prevents us from living in our present reality. Trust me when I say you will need all your energy to fight what you are dealing with in the present—not the past. Once you realize this, your ability to heal will be enhanced.

6. Don't wait for someone to inform you. John and I made that mistake until I was well into recovery. Being proactive and seeking support groups and programs empowers you and serves as a reminder that you *can* control some of the process. Talk to those who have been through it. They will most likely know of many community resources and share valuable insights about what was helpful for them. Use their knowledge for your own benefit while keeping in mind that what worked for one person may not work for you.

CHAPTER 3B: JOHN

Bald Is Beautiful!

I'll Cut Mine Too

"I'll shave my head when you lose your hair." I told Sherri that several times. I just wanted her to know she wouldn't be alone. Certainly, it is not unique or new; you always hear about people who make an event of the hair loss from chemotherapy. Spouses, children, coworkers, friends, and relatives will all cut off their hair as a sign of support and solidarity for their loved ones.

Sherri said there was no point in it and me keeping my hair represented some normalcy.

The fateful day was coming. She knew it, and I knew it There was going to be that day when Sherri would be styling her hair in the morning, and as she was blow-drying it, some would fall out. Or maybe she would wake up and find clumps on her pillow. Or worse, she would notice it plastered to her hands as she was washing her hair. I didn't know where, and I didn't know when, but I knew it was coming.

In fact, foolishly, a part of me thought it might not be all that traumatic. Seems like everyone already knows their hair will fall out from chemo. People throw parties, have fundraisers, and post it all over social media. There are all kinds of adornments for bald heads: stocking hats, headbands, wraps, and scarves. You see bald patients used in ads and even on billboards.

I thought, *When it happens, I'll just surprise her with all kinds of nice things for her to wear on her head.* Heck, her treatments started at the end of June with the hottest weather on the horizon. Sherri would not even need anything on her head. In fact, she might find being bald in the summer months more comfortable. My mission would be to make her baldness something special that she could embrace rather than dread and feel ashamed of. Boy, was I way, *way* off on that.

Cut It Off—Now!

Summer was moving along, and Sherri had just finished her second chemotherapy treatment. I was already attending summer football workouts, and the season was just around the corner.

On a July day, when Sherri was about a week out from going back into the hospital for round 3 of treatment, I was puttering around in the garage. She came out of the house with tears rolling down her face. It had begun; the hair was coming out by the handful. We had talked in advance and had a plan. When this day finally came, she would be having her hair cut off to not endure the fallout.

I had told her I would cut it for her, but she did not want that. Her hairstylist had promised to do it and even offered to come to our house so Sherri would not have to have it all cut off in public. I was caught off guard when she came out to the garage and said, "Cut it off—now!" I asked her if she was sure and reminded her that she had wanted her stylist to do it. She had no desire to wait and was quite emphatic about it. So, like I had done for my sons when they were younger, I was going to buzz Sherri's hair off as short as my "dad clippers" would allow.

Sherri was growing noticeably quiet as I set up the stool and got out the apron to wrap around her. When the clippers started to hum, it opened the floodgates open—and Sherri began to sob. The tears were flowing down her cheeks, and the freshly cut hair was sticking to her skin.

I stopped and asked if she was sure she wanted me to continue, and the answer was yes. Before I knew it, I had tears rolling down my face. I was not prepared for—nor did I expect—the burst of emotion from either of us. Up to that point, I had remained strong and solid as a rock emotionally. The rock cracked a bit that day. This was a harsh dose of the reality of our situation.

So, what did I do? I did what any caregiver should do. I hugged her, held her, hugged her some more, and then I finished cutting. The whole thing was gut-wrenching, and I had misjudged how this would feel for Sherri—and for myself. You can talk all you want about how you know this is going to happen and that you will be ready, but the truth is that you may not be. I suppose it is like anything else. I have always believed that a person truly does not know how they will react in a crisis until they find themselves in one for the first time.

I cannot say how I would have reacted because it wasn't me losing the hair. A woman's hair is part of who she is. Traditionally, women spend way more time and money on their hair than men. This is not being sexist; it is just facts. My mother, even at ninety-three, goes to the beauty salon once a week to get her hair done.

Naivete

So now I can see how ridiculous it was to think this would be easy for her and that she would act is if it were nothing. What a fool I was; it totally reshaped my approach to everything, but I don't know if I realized the impact this whole cancer thing had on me at that time. I can look back and say with certainty that I became much more aware of how every appointment, each poke from a needle, the scars from surgery, the weight loss, and the bloating from steroids would affect her emotionally and mentally.

As soon as I finished cutting off all her hair, I softly brushed off her scalp and massaged it a little bit. I stepped back, and I made sure to tell her how beautiful she looked.

She got up, still in tears, wiped her face, and ran to look at herself in a mirror. All she could muster up was: "Oh my God. I look like my dad!" She was sobbing.

We can laugh at that now. Sherri's dad Bill is as bald as a cue ball and always called people out when they dropped "cheap bald jokes" on him. In the moment, it was nothing to laugh at.

She said, "Now everyone will know and only see me as a cancer patient."

I suppose there is a lot of truth to that. I reassured her that people who know her and love her were not suddenly going to look at her differently. They wouldn't think, "Oh no, Sherri has cancer—look at her."

I was way off there. In truth, people did look at her differently as a bald cancer patient. As a caregiver, I helped her stand tall and proud regardless of her outward physical appearance. Yes, once again, until a person either has cancer or is a caregiver for someone who does, they will not truly understand what people go through. I was one of those ignorant people. This experience is a good lesson to all: everything that happens to someone undergoing a traumatic, life-changing, or life-threatening experience matters and will have some sort of consequence. The physical will affect the mental and the emotional. It is inevitable. Sure, things can be overcome, but in the moment, when the action is real, you must be ready for the expected *and* the unexpected. Sometimes there is nothing to say to make it better—just listen and be there.

The Wig

The week the hair came out, we got Sherri into a boutique for wigs. I remember sitting back out of the way and realizing that I was experiencing one of those moments that will always be vividly clear in my memories. There was the love of my life, my best friend, the mother of our children, sitting in a salon chair, trying to regain some of who she was before cancer. I welled up, but I fought the tears for fear of triggering Sherri's emotions.

As I watched all this, I wondered about so many random questions. *How long will it take to get through all this? Will she make it? When will her hair grow back? Will we get back to normalcy?*

When she caught my eye in the mirror, I smiled and nodded and gave her a thumbs-up. But inside, I was a mess. I knew I had to be strong and exude positivity and confidence. Every day, she was asking herself how this was going to end. I made sure to emphasize the confidence of the medical team that everything was going just fine, and that a year from then, it would all be a memory.

Bald Is Beautiful!

Every day thereafter, I rubbed her head and told her I loved the bald look, which was not a lie. She looked great with it! She thought I was nuts and just saying it to say it, but I truly found her baldness to be beautiful. She really hated wearing the wig. I only remember a few outings when she actually wore her wig. I know she had it on at my dad's funeral. He died from his own battle with lymphoma while Sherri was undergoing treatments. That was a rough stretch. Sherri had been going through some challenging issues and complications as he was failing in health. In fact, there was a gap in the treatments due to those complications. In that gap period, her hair started to grow back, but it was not looking good. She was quite self-conscious when it grew back in patches of black and white. I know Sherri was talking right away about having to color it, but that never came to be.

Once they rebooted the chemo, all the hair came out again—but it was not traumatic like before. A few months later, when all the treatments were stopped for good and recovery was the name of the game, her hair came back with curls. I gotta say, I totally loved her curls. Sexy!

Takeaways

1. Here we go again. Until it happens to you, you won't fully comprehend. What a fool I was thinking Sherri was ready for the hair loss. Knowing didn't matter, and I had no idea it would be so emotional for me either. Caregivers, nothing about this will be easy. There is always something new waiting at the next turn. That is what you need to know and prepare for.

2. Solidarity! Some make an event of losing their hair from chemo or even turn it into a party or social media event. That was not Sherri's style. Yes, I would have shaved my head in solidarity, but solidarity doesn't mean we all look the same. It means standing together in unity. Respecting her wishes in keeping this private and keeping my hair was my solidarity with her.

3. I love my "bald girl." Self-esteem gets shot to hell for some cancer patients. How we see and feel about ourselves is what we believe we project to the world. You will need to show unquestionable support throughout this. So, massage the bald head, embrace the changes, and show your loved one nothing but unconditional love and appreciation. Bring the value to their lives that they may be questioning.

CHAPTER 4A: SHERRI

Ch-ch-ch-ch-changes

My Body, Ravaged

Three completed rounds of chemotherapy marked the halfway point of treatments, and the doctor scheduled me for a PET scan to determine how effective the treatment had been thus far. Although I was nervous, my body was feeling pretty well physically, all things considered. Definitely not nearly as bad as I expected to feel during treatments. But then the doctor told us the results were "concerning," and shockwaves pummeled me. Apparently, from a purely lymphoma standpoint, the PET scan looked good. However, now there were new patches on my lungs and spleen. They weren't sure if it was a new form of cancer or an infection or if my immune system was attacking itself. Immediately labs were drawn, I was admitted, and more scans and scopes were scheduled.

Just Breathe

These new nodules made the doctors scratch their heads, not knowing what they were dealing with. Round 4 of chemotherapy was put on a temporary hold so they could focus on these mystery spots. While in the hospital, I kept doing my thing. I continued walking laps and taking short strolls outside to keep sane mentally. Something wasn't right, as over the course of the week, I was getting progressively slower and had more difficulty breathing. My inspirometer exercises were diminishing. An inspirometer is a lung-strengthening device where patients are encouraged to take deep inhalations making a ping-pong type ball rise in a tube. My oxygen saturation "O2 sats," a measurement of the oxygen in the bloodstream that is taken by placing a clip apparatus on your fingernail, were dropping. This number should have been in the mid-nineties. For most people, it will be high nineties or even one hundred. Within a day or two, my numbers were dipping into the eighties. The doctors still didn't know which way to go with treatment.

Trapped in uncertainty and feeling like a prisoner in that hospital, I needed to escape. John and I took a long walk outside, and we snuck out onto the OSU campus. The struggle to walk and breathe became real. I was wheezing and getting lightheaded along the way. My God, would we make it back to the hospital, which now seemed miles away? We both were getting nervous, but slowly and methodically, we got back. John grabbed a wheelchair from the lobby to take me back to my room.

By that evening, I had to be placed on continuous oxygen with a cannula in my nose. *Three months ago, I didn't know I had cancer—and now I'm stuck in bed on oxygen? Where did my life go?* To this day, during routine checkups, when an O2 sat device is clipped to my finger, I start gulping in large breaths of air, hoping the numbers will be high. It scares me—no, it absolutely petrifies me—that the reading will flash a number in the low nineties, indicating a possible decrease in lung efficiency.

Emergency Response Team

Have you ever not been able to breathe? The shortness of breath was getting worse. I felt like I was slowly suffocating. The resulting fear made the possibility of death seem real. I felt like a board was on my chest with rocks being piled on. I was slowly suffocating.

My nurse looked quite concerned. Her usual cheerful, fun demeanor became very businesslike and methodical, and after checking me over, she pulled the trigger, calling a respiratory emergency, which brought an emergency response team (ERT) to my room. Within seconds, my room was buzzing like a hive. People showed up out of nowhere, and someone rolled in a ventilator.

They all went right to work like a well-oiled machine. An arterial line was put in my arm, and all sorts of devices and wires were attached to me.

Someone I had never seen before entered the room and asked, "Do you wish to be resuscitated should your heart stop or you stop breathing?"

I couldn't grasp what was being asked. Then I just stopped listening and went numb. Imagine being asked that fateful question. This is a do not resuscitate question! I yelled out as loud as I could with a mask over my face, "Please do everything! I'm not ready to die!"

Scared and at the same time confused, my mind was racing. Was this really happening to me? It felt like a dream because even though scared, I felt calm in my body while the people all around me were shouting orders, poking, and prodding me. John was actually working that day, so I was alone. At this point, I have no recollection of what took place; they must have sedated me. Coming out of it, I awoke in an intensive care stepdown unit with no ventilator. Thank God for that!

You Are Taking Out My What?

It had been a solid week in the hospital. Round 4 of chemo never happened. I lost my ability to breathe without the assistance of oxygen, an ERT save my life, and now? Now they want my spleen! After being stabilized for a few days, it was decided the best course of action was to suspend chemo again and instead remove my spleen due to those new spots found on the PET scan. Oh no! Is it spreading? I was mortified. There was little time to consider options, and I signed the consent for surgery. The doctors were concerned about doing another lung biopsy and didn't want to remove more lung tissue, so the spleen it was.

A Splenectomy

The removal of my spleen happened quickly. At the time, it was seemingly uneventful (well, except for the fact that I lost my spleen). Looking back, I regret agreeing so quickly to the surgery. Hindsight is twenty-twenty, and what was about to follow would make anyone question the hasty decision. Additionally, the spleen is an important part of the immune system—and God knows my immune system was already a mess. But after the respiratory emergency, all the chemo drugs, pain meds, sleeping pills, and outright fear and exhaustion, the questions asked by a clear mind just didn't come to me. We knew they needed to find out what was going on, and I probably would have jumped off a cliff if they said it would cure me. These people—my team and the James staff—all of them wrapped together were my lifeline, and anything they said I was willing to do if it meant saving my life. Honestly,

45

by that stage of the game, I all but forgot I was a nurse and didn't think anymore with my normally scientific, inquisitive mind.

A Bigger Problem

Post splenectomy, being discharged and home, sleeping in my own bed, was wonderful. Waking up the next morning, I took about twenty steps and was hit with an excruciating pain that caused me to double over. The pain wouldn't let up. The decision was made to call the rescue squad because I couldn't even walk to the car. Tears came fast and furiously because I did not want to go back to the hospital! I had just left and had no desire to go back, especially if it meant finding out something else terrible was wrong with me.

We live a block from a fire station, so hearing sirens and seeing rescue vehicles go whizzing by the house happens a lot. Generally, my mind gives it a passing thought. On any given day, we encounter a life squad or fire truck on the road, pull to the side, and then move on; if it doesn't affect us, we dismiss it inconsequentially. But this time, when the sirens get closer and closer to your home, knowing they are coming for you, this brings a whole new awareness to what the sirens really mean.

The EMTs arrived and loaded me up for a ride back to the hospital. It was as if the hospital was really my home, and I was just visiting what I used to call home. The ride in the ambulance was such an odd reality. The EMTs saw me as this frail, bald, cancer patient in excruciating pain. In my mind, I still envisioned my old self from years gone by: the strong, fit nurse who used to work alongside these people saving lives when I worked in the ER. Yet here I was trapped in a body that needed saving. I wanted to scream, "This isn't really me!"

After more scans and tests a new diagnosis entered the ring: a nicked colon and a bowel obstruction.

Sherri, Meet Your New Companion.

Surgery it is! They whisked me out of that room like the wind. After surgery, I woke up in the intensive care unit. Devastated is how to best describe my emotions waking up in the ICU, only to discover their solution to the obstruction resulted in a colostomy. My God, I now have a hole in my abdomen and a plastic bag to catch my excrement. Yet another piece of my body and a vital function were gone. What would be next?

Many hours after surgery, my GI system kicked in, and I awoke only to find what felt like an "alien" attached to my abdomen. I found the bag filled to capacity with gas and liquid stool, about to burst. Pushing the call button in a state of panic, I didn't know what in the hell was going on. This can't be real; nothing was registering. Subconsciously though, I knew this meant the start of a new way of life for me. The nurse helped me to the bathroom to empty this toxic mess. The bag opened over the toilet with such force it exploded all over me, the nurse, and the bathroom. Just awful. I was in tears, but she didn't bat an eye. It was as if this was perfectly normal. For that, I thank her and am eternally grateful. God bless those nurses. They were constantly emptying and measuring poop and urine with smiles on their faces.

The ostomy nurses must have all been members of their schools' pep squads or cheerleading teams in their younger days because they would come into the room and tell me how *great* the whole colostomy experience was and how fashionable it can be. I was even given a complimentary designer bag to wear over it. Who knew!? A whole designer line of fashionable colostomy bag covers.

Living with My New Friend "Betty"

A person can lead a very normal and active life with an ostomy bag. If you have to choose between a colostomy bag or death, the bag is the obvious choice! My mind was having difficulty processing this new "appendage." Not being able to prepare myself that the splenectomy would result in a colostomy added to the grief and difficulty coping. The doctor did say one little thing that did not get by me: hopefully it would be temporary. Yep, he said it. Everyone in the room heard it. He said *temporary*. This could be reversed. OK, so let's put it on the calendar!

As I quickly came to find out, this little "lady" had a mind of her own. Deciding, since I was apparently stuck with her, it might be better to become friends, she was aptly named "Betty." "Betty Poop" was her formal name (if you have heard of a very old cartoon character Betty Boop, then you know where I got the name). Betty was a messy gal. She liked to leak all around the seal at the stoma (the attachment point on my body) and get on my clothes. She would fill up with poo at the most inopportune times. She also offered surprise "puffs" of gas that filled the bag like it was a party balloon. Betty was often full of shit!

Book the Damn Surgery!

Yes! My persistence with the gastro surgeon finally paid off. Surgery was finally scheduled for removal of the colostomy. Betty and I were going to be parting ways after only two months of being together. I was ecstatic, and we had the date highlighted and bolded on our calendars. Chemo had been placed on hold during this particular ordeal. Meanwhile, doctors were dissecting the spleen and trying to figure out what the new spots on my lungs and spleen were.

I came to appreciate and respect how strong people are who aren't as lucky to have their ostomy be temporary. There is a large population out there who live with these challenges every day for the rest of their lives. And they live life to the fullest extent that they can. I am very humbled by their perseverance.

I Want to Go "Home."

So much of that year I was reminded of Dorothy's iconic line from 1939 film *The Wizard of Oz*. I kept thinking, *There's no place like home*. Oh, how badly I wanted to be at home. Even when I was physically in our house, I still had this longing for "home." What I have come to realize about this yearning and desire was "home" is not a place; it is more the sense of comfort, love, and security that I used to know. The little things often taken for granted and the boring mundane day-to-day routines—I wanted it all back. Home meant my life, my family, my career, my hobbies, and all the wonderful emotions that go with them.

Sometimes it was hard to remember the last time I felt truly "home." Coming through all of this and making it to the other side has helped me really appreciate and savor the little things. When you are facing a life-threatening illness, you quickly learn to separate what is important from what really doesn't matter. Being able to let things go is very liberating emotionally and even physically; lifting the weight of self-imposed baggage lightens the stress we carry.

I would never wish cancer on anyone, but for everyone and anyone, I would wish the experience of realizing what matters and what doesn't matter at such a raw emotional level. This experience has blessed me with newfound strength and a deeper sense of empathy. Being lucky and blessed to have survived this and the ability to understand and connect with so many others is something to be grateful for.

My Happy Place

Most of the time during my treatment, I slept in a spare bedroom. The room was adjacent to our master bedroom, and I liked my space. This room has a double patio door and its own little balcony that overlooks the pond we live on. In the mornings, this room gets a full-on view when we get a beautiful sunrise.

This room became a place of peace and calm for me, and I looked forward to going to bed surrounded by a Zen-like space followed by mornings that were always a new day of hope. Positive vibes filled the room as it overlooked the pond and brought the beauty of a new day. Bedtime always brought a ritual of John tucking me in for the night. Simple gestures like that are not complicated or grand, but they are full of complete love. His love was unconditional, unquestionable, and endless. Love pulled me through this awful time.

Having this private, personal space gave me a place for rest and healing that was all my own. This small but positive force gave me an emotional boost of peace and hope. The space was set up and created by me, filled with things that made my heart happy. The room was immersed in scents from soothing essential oils being diffused, calming colors on the walls, relaxing lighting, uplifting photos, and motivational quotes. Being in this space brought pure joy.

Vacation Over, Back to Chemo

Now that Betty Poop was out of my life, the colostomy having been reversed, it was time to return to the trenches of chemotherapy! Not so fast! Wanting to join the party, my bladder got an infection—a urinary tract infection (UTI) that wiped me out. Just getting in a car was brutally difficult and took all the energy I could muster. But it was necessary to keep moving and using my body. This setback was mentally defeating in spite of all the "big" stuff I had dealt with. This was just a common UTI, but it was destroying me.

Even though at times, you may wonder if the fight is worth it, all I can say is never give up! There were days when I told myself "OK, don't give up for the next minute and then the next minute," and on and on it went until I was able to bring myself back to a better place. Remaining steadfast in my attitude, I swore I was not going to let any of this define me or diminish me. Despite the complications, I persevered and was finally cleared to continue chemotherapy.

"Ho-Ho-How Did This Happen?"

Back on the sixteenth floor at the James, all nestled into my little corner of the hospital, the five inpatient days of chemotherapy went along uneventfully. Naturally, this didn't last, and over the two weeks between treatments that followed, all hell broke loose again. Dizzy spells and general lightheadedness upon standing would not subside. Add in nausea and diarrhea—and what a holiday recipe! Christmas was almost here, and I was a mess. The days leading up to Christmas can only be described as a catatonic blur; what happened over the course of almost two weeks are only known to me through John and our family. I literally have no memory of almost two weeks of my life due to mental deterioration.

The loss of the precious memories, knowing that all my boys were home for the holidays and there is no recall of anything, remains one of the hardest aspects of my cancer journey. Nick, our oldest son, and his wife, Emily, even came home from Germany for a week. But I only know that through photos. It was as if I was asleep for that entire time.

My team finally concluded that the mental deterioration was a combination of different but powerful medications that were contradicting and interacting with each other, and the chemistry of it all was disastrous mentally and physically to my mind and body. My body was beaten down, but I still had two more rounds of chemo to endure. The New Year was only a few days away when I was released from the Christmas chaos. After a short reprieve, round 5 would begin.

An Unfortunate Chain of Events

I was admitted for round 5, but I entered the hospital with a headache, coughs, and the signs of some sort of infection. Worse yet, let's add loss of hearing to the list. Two days later, after a bombardment of antibiotics and fluids, my body stabilized, and the oncologist was ready to forge on with round 5 of chemotherapy. We understood that they had to stay on the timeline for the chemo to do its job, but I was ready to be done. Were the doctors, like me, wondering if my body could take it anymore? Apparently not—since we went forward with the treatment. This may be hard to believe, but round 5 of chemo went off without any glitches, and they sent me home to recover. Within two days, everything went south again. I am really not sure how things could get worse, but well, you know it seemed to be a trend.

I Am Not a Mummy!

The whole chain of events began with a sudden drop in blood pressure. Dizziness and fevers had been riddling my body for a few days. At every attempt to stand, my blood pressure dropped drastically. I was deteriorating quickly, so off we went to the hospital. A two-week stretch at the James would feel like a lifetime. This stay would test my mental, physical, and emotional strength more than any other part of this ordeal, stretching me so thin that by discharge, I could not walk without the assistance of a gait belt or walker.

As one would expect, several blood tests were done, including special cultures that were drawn every time I developed a fever. My hearing was still not restored. John would have to look right at me and be very close to me for me to know what was being said. We don't realize how important our senses are and can take them for granted. Not being able to hear doctors or staff was a new level of fright and frustration.

Between the incredibly bad sinus infection and the loss of my hearing, the team decided to bring in ear, nose, and throat doctors (ENT) to start digging around my head. A young resident would come to my room both morning and night to stick a probe up my nose. Actually, it felt like he was digging into my brain for an alien lodged somewhere up there. Have you ever seen a documentary on Egyptian mummification? They go up the nose with a hook and yank the brains out of the corpse! Well, that is what it felt like during that procedure. The ENT doctor said they were looking for some type of brain-eating bacteria. Wait, what? I was trying to understand and process all of this while not being able to hear, and the nurses would help interpret what was being said.

Enter Neurology

Just for fun, two more scans were ordered, once again confirming the sinus infection, but they were not sure what type of microbe was causing the infection. The second scan was an MRI of the brain which brought a new "player" to the table. And not a welcome one.

The day the neurologist who read the brain MRI walked into the room, it felt like he was pushing me off a cliff. Now, mind you, I had never met or even seen him before. He walked right in and proceeded to spring the news on me that there were two spots on my brain, which he believed were malignant brain cancer. *Oh. My. God! This cannot be happening to me!* My husband had not arrived yet from work. My hearing was all but nonexistent, all I could make out was "you have malignant brain cancer." I couldn't even ask questions because I couldn't hear the answers. This news sent me spiraling into one of the biggest meltdowns since the diagnosis. The nurse sedated me just to calm my shaking body. I don't remember any of that evening other than John holding me.

Blood tests continued throughout the whole ordeal. Unfortunately for me, there was nothing jumping out at them, and they were unable to pinpoint why my blood pressure kept dropping and the high fevers persisted, leaving me weak and unable to stand. For my safety, the nurses activated the bed alarm, forbidding me from getting up alone, and I was forced to use a bedside commode since getting to the bathroom was impossible. This was incredibly defeating since the independence I had fought so hard to maintain was gone. I was not well, very feeble, and just so terribly weak. I must have looked awful because one day, out of the blue, an eager resident asked me to verify whether or not I wanted to be saved should I go into cardiac arrest—and did I want them to do everything possible to save me? Are you kidding me? Hell, yes! It didn't take much thought to give him that answer.

Winning the Lottery

Finally, during this two-week ordeal, the lab had a hit from all the tests and cultures. One of the blood cultures came back showing a fungal infection called aspergillosis, and it apparently had penetrated the brain. This was like hitting all the numbers on the lottery. We had an answer! Aspergillus is a fungus found all over the world and around us everywhere. Normally it has no effect on people with healthy immune systems. Obviously, that wasn't me.

An IV antifungal medication was started, and after just a couple infusions I started feeling better. Life and energy started coming back. My blood pressure stabilized, the fevers started coming down, and the lightheadedness went away. And whoopee! My hearing returned, and the congestion subsided. The oncologist, infectious disease doctor, and the pathologist all felt the brain lesions were part of this aspergillosis infection. However, my "good friend" the neurologist held tight to his belief that I had brain cancer. Why he was holding onto this potential diagnosis is beyond me, but I was not happy to have this hanging over my head.

The plan was to wait and see if the antifungal meds worked and then repeat a brain MRI in a couple months, which may as well have been an eternity. Keeping the "brain cancer demon" out of my mind was incredibly tough. The bottom had fallen out from under me so many times already that it was as if I was living my life on thin ice. All I could do was wait anxiously until the next brain MRI.

Learning to Walk Again

This hospitalization took its toll. The degree of deterioration in my body left me so weak that I needed a walker and gait belt to get around. A gait belt is like a heavy-duty belt that helps provide stability for walking assistance. Nevertheless, I did hold on to my determination and continued to wear my battle gear of a running shirt and yoga pants or running shorts. Getting better was a job, and I had to look the part. Everyone would know I meant business.

Physical therapy and occupational therapy worked with me right there in the hospital room and then in the halls once I was strong enough. Eventually, it was decided I could go home. I was prescribed an oral antifungal medication, given orders to continue with PT and OT, and one more thing was mentioned. It's over!

It's Over

My oncologist came in the room before they discharged me, sat down, and told me I would not be receiving the sixth round of chemotherapy. What? Is it not working?

Blinking and doing a double take, when it finally registered with me what he said, I welled up with emotion. In fact, it was a major sigh of relief that came out as it was explained that he didn't want to risk any further complications. It was great news and at the same time quite scary. Being a very driven, "I must complete the task" type of person, it concerned me that we would not finish the course of treatment. Was this a shortcut that could cost me my life? What if all the lymphoma was not eradicated?

Then he said with certainty that the lymphoma was gone and that the six rounds was more of a protocol and not so much a definite rule. It was gone! My brain was running at full speed, trying to process this. All along, I had complete trust and confidence in him—he had gotten me through so many complications—and no way was I going to lose faith now. Being at peace with the decision, it was time to go home for good.

Going Home to an Uncertain Future

Even though I didn't believe it at the time, leaving the hospital on this occasion was actually closing the door to my cancer treatments. Yes, chemo was over, but was it really over? With so many complications throughout this ordeal, part of me doubted it. When the door opened to leave the hospital, it was not the bright sunny skies that I envisioned would be waiting for me. Instead, the door opened to a long tunnel of uncertainty. The tunnel was dark with many turns and no lights to guide me to the end. I did not know where it would lead. This road to recovery would be a labyrinth without a map. Barely able to walk and unable to recognize myself anymore, I went home with mixed messages.

Those messages came from different sources. First, my oncology team says "Cancer gone! See you in a month at the follow up."

Next, the infectious disease doctor would not definitively say aspergillosis was the source of my infection. He said, "Well, we will see what happens—you'll either get better or worse." His statement took the wind out of my sails. And there is this neurologist who did more than take the wind away; he sunk my boat. He would not let go of his gut feeling that I had brain cancer. For God's sake, what was I supposed to believe and have faith in? I cannot emphasize enough how I was feeling both euphoric yet defeated at the same time; my mind was on overload.

Seeking that perfect ending to all of this, I was left with no ending at all. Just uncertainty. I had a choice at this fork in the road: take the easier path and succumb and be debilitated by fear or choose a path of strength, hope, and optimism. Though some days it was more difficult than others, in my heart, I knew the cancer was gone. Whatever choice I made was going to define me. Hope and optimism were my choice.

Two months later, another brain MRI showed there was significant improvement—and the spots on my brain were diminished. Guess what, Dr. Neuro, you were wrong! This confirmed the brain lesions were a fungal infection and the medication prescribed was doing its job. Only then was I finally able to grasp onto the idea that maybe, just maybe, the cancer threat was gone. It was more hope than belief, but hope is what kept me alive and fighting all along.

So, I'm cured. Now what? Recovery is going to be an entirely new animal.

Lessons Learned

1. Cancer sucks. You can say it a thousand times, and it never loses meaning.
2. This is going to be hard. If you are in it, you already know this. Knowing is empowering. Prepare for the worst and strive for the best.
3. Have faith and always keep hope alive. Many survivors write about hope and faith; these were indeed a major part of my victory. I found comfort in the army of prayer warriors out there behind me. God gave me inner strength that I didn't know I had. Rely on your higher power for the strength to fight and heal.

4. Your body can withstand way more than you think. We humans are a powerful species, and it is utterly amazing what our bodies can endure and bounce back from. You have incredible inner strength that you may never have tapped into.

5. Create your own personal space at home. A place of healing, calm, and peace. Design an area that is all you with your creature comforts, favorite pictures, favorite smells, a warm blanket, and anything else that warms your heart. This will be your place of ease that allows your mind, body, and spirit to use their powers to heal you.

6. Worry about what you can control: your attitude, your mind, and your faith. You can control getting up in the morning, what you wear, and what you eat. Make the decisions you can make. You have choices.

7. How do you want to be defined? You are in control. Don't let what is out of your control define you and diminish you.

8. Find what brings you inner peace and joy. Surrounding myself with music helped me endure many of the painful tests and the long days. I made playlists that included songs offering powerful positive messages that helped me find strength even when I didn't know if I could go on.

CHAPTER 4B: JOHN

Keep Calm and Carry On— You Have No Other Choice

Could Anything Else Go Wrong?

Sometime well into recovery, and unbeknownst to me, Sherri nominated me to receive a special award for caregivers. It was sponsored by the Stefanie Spielman Breast Cancer Research Foundation at OSU. Attending a celebration of life tailgate party one fall afternoon, we were sitting with an incredibly special group of people; the group of truly great and amazing people were connected to us through the James and OSU.

It was my fellow caregiver award recipients and their survivors, along with the Spielman family and foundation organizers. Tragically, one of our fellow survivors was not present as he had developed a spiking fever the night before and was admitted to the hospital. That brought it all back for me. I was terribly sad for our new friends and was reminded how important it is to live every day fully.

During the tailgate, I found myself revisiting our journey with a few others. Instantly, it all come rushing back—that time after Sherri's third round of chemo when we spiraled into the worst time of our lives. It was a test of faith, internal strength, commitment, and the ability to effectively function in crisis. Put your seat belt on, and here we go!

Follow the Plan. Stay the Course.

But what do we do when things go awry? We adjust, and we adapt!

In the football world, when there is a game plan in place, it needs to be followed and executed. Coaches will study film, analyze statistics, and scrutinize players and their techniques, looking for clues and tendencies to help their own players be victorious on the field. The culmination of all this work is assembling a game plan that is designed to put the players in the best position to have success and win. At least that is what is supposed to happen.

Sherri's oncology team set out to do just that. They took all their knowledge, experience, and years of research, carefully gathered key information on Sherri specifically, and then assembled a plan they confidently believed would result in her survival and a win over cancer. And when they explained the plan, it was one we had no trouble buying into. Buy-in is pivotal if a game plan is to be successful. All the parties and players involved must be committed and willingly follow the plan, trust the plan, and regardless of circumstances, stick to the plan. All preparations and practice are tailored to this end. Now it was time to put the plan in motion.

Game day! Fast forward to kickoff, or in Sherri's case, day 1 of treatment. The plan was put into play. And oh, what a first half! Chemotherapy was administered, and for three rounds, everything went exactly as planned. Despite being administered some seriously potent and compounding chemical concoctions each round, Sherri handled it like a champion. At the end of round 3, things were looking great. Sherri and her team were kicking lymphoma's ass.

Halftime. If it were a football game, we would head to the locker room, and the coaches would meet, review successes and failures, adjust and make changes, review it all with the players, and then go win the game. So, what was our second-half game plan for treatment? Everything seemed to be working, so why change? It was simple: continue the onslaught and eradicate the cancer. By the end of "regulation" in this "game," Sherri would be the outright victor and could go home to recover and recuperate. Ah, but alas, sometimes plans go awry. Awry? How about obliterated as a better description?

A Full-Time Job

Caregiving for a loved one is a full-time job. The folks out there in the world who are career caregivers for the sick and handicapped, the elderly, and the dying deserve medals of courage and bravery. I don't know how I could face that as a career day in and day out. While it may be true that to professionals, it is a job—and they must detach themselves from the emotional side of things—that must be terribly difficult. When caregiving for your spouse, a child, a parent, or someone very close, there is no going home at the end of the day, detaching yourself, and having a personal life. It is nonstop from the morning alarm clock buzzer to the "nap" that serves as a night's sleep. Caregiving is 24-7, and you will bear the rank of caregiver the rest of your life.

During the first three rounds of chemotherapy, it was a smooth experience being Sherri's primary caregiver. To make sure everything was in place for Sherri's time at home, we developed a system of packing her things for the hospital stays. We had a suitcase ready—just as we did when she was close to the delivery dates of our sons. I had baskets and bags of comforts and reminders of home to put in her hospital room: family photos, cards she had received, motivational signs, and her favorite throw blankets. Just call me "Mr. Efficiency." It was down to a precise science. Cancer had nothing on us—until that mid-treatment PET scan threw everything upside down.

Suck It Up, John

There are days when I look back collectively on the many complications Sherri was slammed with and seriously wonder how the hell she made it *and* how the hell we both managed to keep it together. I'm not exactly patting myself on the back here, but I went on autopilot so often that I never really allowed my emotions to fully expose themselves. This was probably not good for my health, but I was not the one facing a killer disease.

Suck it up, John, and be the husband she needs, I would often tell myself. It was simply necessary to put my emotions, my anxiety, and my absolute dread into a little box and lock the lid. Coming unglued was not an option. Sherri needed a serious rock, more like a boulder, to be there for her. An emotionally unstable caregiver would be no good for her. Nevertheless, I experienced great anxiety and fear. Emotional attachment is such a powerful memory trigger. I recall almost everything that happened, and it triggers those emotions all over again each time those memories surface. They might not be as powerful as they once were, but they are powerful enough.

Most of the time, I held it together, but there was one small breakdown at school. A close teacher friend was asking how things were going for Sherri, and I kind of lost it. I hugged her and just sobbed for a few seconds. I needed that release. Other than that, I just kept on going and going, doing everything necessary to be an efficient and effective caregiver. The Energizer Bunny has nothing on me.

Uniquely prepared

A post I once saw on social media said we should be so busy that we don't have time to be sad. Wow. That described my life to the letter in those days. In fact, that describes my career. As a head football coach, the responsibilities are endless—and there really is no off-season. Over the years, instead of relaxing and enjoying the off-season, I was always in coaching mode, and no matter where we were, I was working on football. It was a love-hate relationship. I thrived on making things work through planning and organization, but the time it took from me was inordinate. However, it absolutely prepared me for this situation: the worst ordeal ever faced in my life.

Be Invincible

The moment Sherri's diagnosis was delivered, all my responsibilities quadrupled. Add to that fact the emotional attachment and strain of watching a loved one grapple with their health and maybe even their mortality, and you have the recipe for a breakdown. No! There was just no way I was going to break down! A breakdown would fail Sherri, and I could not fail the love of my life. There are no eloquent quotes from psychology journals here, and I cannot cite individuals who went through similar experiences to affirm my strategies. There was no time for looking into that. I didn't have time to do jack squat except take care of my wife, our home, our finances, go to work, keep family and friends informed, and take care of anything else that would come up.

There was no way in hell cancer would beat Sherri, and there was no way in hell her caregiver would fail her. That was my mindset. As a coach, my teams faced many opponents over the years who grossly outmatched them in size, speed, and experience. I relished those games. It was a chance to instill a mindset in young men that no opponent is unbeatable. Cancer is one of those opponents. It is powerful, it moves fast, and it is relentless. Cancer doesn't fight fair. Cancer is formidable and, generally speaking, anyone who has it is the underdog initially. But Sherri's cancer was up against a woman whose love, energy, and will to live was and is incredibly strong. It was up against her team and her caregivers. It was time to fight!

Being There

When a PET scan showed new developments, Sherri's team sprang into action. As we found out during the process, Sherri was both an anomaly and a celebrity at the James. The staff coming and going in her room at times was constant. When she developed all her complications, she became the discussion piece in the OSU Oncology Department. Her team often confided to me that they were conferring with colleagues regularly when it came to Sherri's care and treatment. Though that did not bring comfort, at least I knew she was going to get the best care they could provide.

Sherri faced several extended stays in the James, and I continued to stay in her room and slept on the couch, which could be extended into a little bed that was long enough for me to stretch out. The patient care assistants (PCAs) who aided the nurses and patients provided me with sheets, blankets, and pillows each time we arrived. They knew me as well as they knew Sherri. I was able to go down to the locker rooms in the basement and shower. She tried to suggest I go home and sleep, but she soon gave up when she knew I would have none of that. And so, throughout the entire ordeal, we both stayed together—no matter what—in our little home away from home: the sixteenth floor of the James Cancer Hospital. She appreciated it immensely, and I would do it all over again. Being there almost full-time aside from work allowed me to fully support her and be that bulldog of a caregiver who asked all the questions and tracked everything.

Helplessness

Responsibility is humbling and is always breathing down your neck. When you are the one in charge, you are truly the *last* person who can lose their composure and have a breakdown. Twenty-three years as a head football coach taught me that. I had to be the one person on the field who did not allow the excitement of a moment to overcome my judgment and clear thinking; this requires calm, composed behavior and controlled emotions. As caregiver, this must be your mantra.

There were multiple key points on my caregiving journey where I had to remain calm. If I had not remained calm, no one would have. Such as the time her nurse called me at school because Sherri had gone into respiratory duress. That was a doozy of a call. Keeping calm was a necessity, but the feelings of helplessness and guilt flowing through my mind were crushing. My heart was in my mouth. In my haste driving to get to Sherri, my mind played out all sorts of scenarios. The worst one was that I would walk in and see Sherri unconscious and on a ventilator or that she didn't make it—and I was not there at the end.

Literally sprinting to the elevator and then her room, I finally arrived. Helpless. Completely helpless. Sherri had a team of people around her. I could only catch glimpses of her between them. Moving around to the far side of the room allowed the chance to get up to her. She had an oxygen mask on, and fear was emanating from her big eyes. I grabbed her hand and told her everything would be OK and that I loved her. Then I stepped back out of the way. At that moment, I knew I had to stay calm and let these folks do their work. I could do nothing except be present. I was helpless and needed to get out of their way.

No one can predict what will happen during illnesses or foresee the complications and setbacks. Being helpless is a horrific feeling. As caregivers, we are solid as a rock for our loved ones, and we become these careful planners who take charge of everything. Though I was confident and feeling strong and reliable, I was not ready for the moments where I could do absolutely nothing to help. What can be predicted is that you will have these bouts with helplessness. All I could do was remain calm, stay positive, focus on the things I could control—like asking questions and noting all that was said and done—and trust the professionals. Expect the unexpected, and when it comes, face it head-on.

More Crisis

What do you do when there is a complication that results from another complication? A surreal chain of events started with a scan showing spots on Sherri's spleen and ended with her bowels emptying into a plastic bag attached to her stomach. Peppered in there were two surgeries, a trip to the emergency room, and one seriously distraught cancer patient.

Expecting the Unexpected Is Not So Easy

I had no way of knowing what was coming. That feeling of helplessness was rising again. They rushed her out so fast for the bowel obstruction surgery and explained little. Nobody told me what the end game of this bowel obstruction was going to be. Did they know and forget to mention it? Or was this a normal, "no big deal" type of procedure? As soon as I signed the waiver, the doctor took off to do the procedure. Since it was well before dawn, there was no one else around to explain the process to me. I just sat there all by myself in that room, enveloped in lonely helplessness—but also frustrated and angry. How had this happened—and why are we dealing with this?

She Has to Wake Up to a Nightmare

Nothing—I repeat, nothing—could have prepared me for what I was told by the surgeon after he finished the procedure or for what I saw as Sherri lay in the intensive care unit at the James. The surgeon explained that he had to remove part of her colon where it had been nicked from the previous splenectomy surgery. He could not reattach it all because there was inflammation in the bowel. In place of a regularly functioning digestive system, Sherri would awake to find her colon now emptying into a colostomy bag attached to her stomach where the colon was attached. She had a bag to catch her feces now, which would no longer come out where it was supposed to. I was absolutely mortified—for her and for me. *How am I going to tell her this? What is going to happen when she wakes up and finds out? Could anything else go wrong for her?*

In the ICU, Sherri was still asleep from the anesthesia. I lifted the blanket and saw the bag. Tears rolled down my face in that moment. This beautiful, amazing woman had so many incisions over the past six months. She handled all of them like a prizefighter. But this? This could take some time.

When her mom and dad came back to the ICU to see her, it was difficult to watch. I watched as they held her hand as she slept. Her mom was very emotional. Her dad wept. It was a moment I won't soon forget. The sight of them looking at their little girl, feeling as helpless as me, was more than I could take. I sat down in a chair in the back of her ICU room and shut my eyes.

Sherri would not wake up for a while. That gave me time to bring myself to a state of calm and to contemplate a series of questions for the surgeon. I knew that once she came to grips with this, she was going to be distraught, angry, depressed—and determined to find a way to get that bag removed and her normal functioning system back.

When she started to come out of the anesthesia, I was filled with a sense of dread about having to tell her the truth. I did not want the doctor or staff to tell her. It had to be me. She woke up and immediately wanted to know where she was. The nasogastric tube was in her nose and down her throat, making talking difficult for her to ask what happened. I explained the events of the night before, followed by what they discovered in surgery. I held her hand and then shakily told her about the colostomy. This was so hard. She wanted to see it. I lifted the blanket, and her reaction tore my heart in two. She was terrified at the sight of it. Though sedated, she sobbed. I just held her hand and said nothing.

How do you make someone feel better about that? You don't just say, "Hey, don't worry. Everything will be fine." I had no idea if it would be. Just be silent and be strong.

Yes, Supporting Means Helping with That Too

The colostomy bag posed some entirely new problems. Sherri was excreting feces out of her bowel into a bag, and it absolutely repulsed her. My role was to help her change it, clean the wound and attachment area, and help her learn to manage it herself. Was it gross? Yes. But what option did I have? This was a major mental and emotional blow to her. My gut told me the doctor was not prepared for the pressure she would place on him to reattach her bowel so they functioned normally.

Sherri was all over the surgeon from the moment she woke up from the colostomy; she was not going to live the rest of her life with a bag. I knew it was a real possibility she might have to, but we both remained vigilant in pestering the doctor about a "reattachment" surgery date. Though I suspect there was reluctance, the gastro surgeon agreed to reverse the colostomy and reattach her digestive tract two months later. She was the most happy and joyous I had seen in ten months when he agreed. We just had to hold tight, be careful at home with germ management and food prep, and keep her healthy. Nothing was going to get in her way. The bag was removed near Thanksgiving. That was a good weekend!

Put Your Emotions in a Box

The complications list just kept growing. Wrong or right, I developed this almost out-of-body reaction to each one. I could not panic and become emotional; my reactions became automatic, almost mechanical. Sherri did plenty of that already. She didn't need a caregiver who lost his wits every time a setback occurred.

As soon as we found out she was having a problem, I went to work. I contacted the oncologist, took her to the hospital, asked all the questions, and documented everything. The issues kept mounting, even while waiting for the reversal of the colostomy. Staying ahead of the complications was the name of the game. We certainly could not foresee what was coming, but by having a plan in place in case of emergency, a way to reach the oncologist anytime and working ahead on bills, finances, and "house stuff," I was able to jump into action faster than a minuteman. "Be prepared" was my motto. That was about to be put to the test

Our Christmas from Hell

Though Sherri was still in treatment, we were looking forward to the holidays. Everyone was going to be home for the first time in a while; it was going to be a special Christmas for sure. Due to her weakened state, getting the house ready for the holidays fell to me almost exclusively. Normalcy is critical, and I was determined to not let all that was going on be an excuse for ignoring the holiday. If anything, normalcy and a great Christmas were more important than ever; the house was going to be decorated inside and out. We needed to celebrate life—not honor the sickness. Turns out it didn't matter if the house was decorated or not. The sickness was going to be heard.

Here are the facts before we get into the holidays event: 1.) Sherri was now on a medication intended to throttle down her immune system from going into overdrive and attacking her body, 2.) she had been recovering from the colostomy reversal, 3.) she had completed three rounds of chemotherapy, 4.) she was battling some infections, 5.) and chemotherapy had just been resumed.

Memories? Sherri has no recollection of what happened. I have had to tell the story to her multiple times. She cannot describe the trauma of that Christmas because it is absent from her memories. Round 4 of chemo went as planned, and Sherri would have the holidays at home. She was ecstatic, and I was thrilled to see her joy when the oncologist said the latest scans showed the treatments were working in eradicating the lymphoma!

Once Sherri was home, she began experiencing the typical post-chemo side effects: nausea, fatigue, exhaustion, and weakness. They zapped her with the most potent dose of the chemo cocktail yet, and it really wiped her out. I was paying close attention to her physically and emotionally. The nausea and fatigue were to be expected after chemo, so I didn't think much of those, but things worsened.

I ran out on Christmas Eve to finish some shopping. When I left for the stores, she was sleeping. Hours later, when I got home, she was still sleeping. No wonder she didn't answer any texts or calls while I was shopping! This was not right. She was foggy and out of sorts. Even when awake, she was so out of it as if in a drug fog. Our oldest and his wife were due in from Germany by early evening. Sherri, though she did not show it, was eager to see them, but the fatigue was overwhelming her. When the kids arrived, she gave hugs and kisses, but she didn't last long. It was their first time seeing her in a year, and I could tell they were really shocked and concerned at how zombielike she seemed. She was so out of it that I took her back upstairs to go to bed. This was not normal. If things were not better the next day, I had a feeling we might need to call the doctor or take her in. What a prophecy!

Christmas Day was a continuation. She was in a fog and as lethargic as could be. I woke her up, helped her shower, and brought her down for dinner. She seemed slightly better for a short time to open gifts, but soon she just wanted to go back to bed. What transpired next was terrifying for me and our family.

When she came downstairs for Christmas dinner, she was moving slowly and clearly out of sorts, and it was like she was not even seeing me. There was a serious delay in her reaction to my statements and questions. Once we all sat down at the table, Sherri just sat there staring into space. At one point, she picked up her plate and was going to pass it around to us as if passing a bowl of potatoes or something. She was mixing all her food together on her plate and staring weirdly into space. She was incoherent and had no idea what she was doing. That was it.

Inside, I was freaking out, but no one knew it. I sprang into action and called the hospital. The doctor called back quickly, asked me a few questions, and said I needed to bring her in immediately. I sat in the back seat as one of our sons drove us to the emergency room. She had no clue what was going on. Once in the ER, it did not take long before she was admitted for yet another extended stay.

Several days later, after tests and monitoring, Sherri began to come out of her fog and gradually became coherent again. She has a gap of nearly two weeks in her memory. Turns out that perfect storm I mentioned was exactly that. The combination of all her medications and the chemo in her body sent her spiraling. She would have to be told the same things over and over because her short-term memory seemed to have stopped working.

To this day, I just melt inside when it comes up. She still gets so emotional about that gap in her memory, and it breaks my heart. When she came across an item she did not recognize, like a scarf, new mittens, or an unopened bottle of perfume, I had to explain that she had received them as gifts for Christmas.

Always Monitoring Her

I notice everything about Sherri as a result of this cancer ordeal. I can tell when she is not feeling up to par or when she is mentally stewing about her health, worried about her coughs, everything. I'm conditioned that way now. Caregivers, all throughout a trauma, really need to watch the patient closely and keep notes, both written and mental, on how they seem to look and feel. I am now, even to this day, always acutely aware of how Sherri feels. Caregiving requires diligence and incredible persistence, and it becomes a habit. This will come into play when Sherri is in recovery and trying to regain her independence, and I just can't seem to get out of her way.

It's Finally Over—At Least This Part

Round 5 of chemo was administered, and that was the end of it; she would not need or receive a sixth round. She was cured of the lymphoma! But when Sherri finally left the James, she could barely walk and was but a shell of even who she was. My wife was using a walker. A walker? Frankly, she was almost weak enough to need a wheelchair full-time. When she fell, I had to help her get up because she had no strength to do it herself. How was she even alive after all that?

Sherri was starting the process of full recovery. Life would get back to normal right away—well, not so fast on that part. But for now, I have her home and can get to the business of helping her get her life back.

Takeaways

1. Caregiving is full time. Period. Just know this.
2. Suck it up and be invincible. They'd do the same for you. No excuses. You *must* be strong.
3. Keep your eyes open all the time. Paying attention to your loved one's cues about how they are feeling is critical and could save their life.
4. Keep calm! If you aren't calm, who will be? You may be the only one who can keep the ship steady and afloat.
5. Expect unexpected complications. You may not know when or what, but ready your mind and decide how you will react. It helps.
6. Have a plan. Make sure you know how you will handle emergencies—no matter where you are when they happen. Crises happen. You cannot predict them, but you can have a protocol for handling them.
7. Make sure all your other duties are done and up-to-date, such as finances and insurance. You won't want all that on your plate when things get dicey.
8. You may have your own crap to deal with outside the trauma going on with your loved one. Put it away in a box for now. Deal with it when you can, but you are now focused 100 percent on your loved one.
9. Compassion. You are going to have to live your life around that word. Be compassionate, no matter how hard it gets. If roles were reversed, wouldn't you want it that way?
10. The little things matter. At the time, I never realized how important just making Sherri feel comfortable and safe was. Tucking her in

at night, adjusting her pillows strategically after one of the many surgeries, protecting her incisions and preventing movements that would cause pain, getting her tea or a light snack, and setting up a Zen place for her to relax—all these caregiving gestures matter. Do them! They bring hope and inspire the will to fight.

PART II

"YOU'RE CURED."
OK, NOW WHAT?

CHAPTER 5A: SHERRI

A Spoonful of Sugar Helps the Medicine Go Down

Optimism Matters: Finding Positivity

Mary Poppins is one of my all-time favorite films. "A Spoonful of Sugar Helps the Medicine Go Down" is a great sing-along, and it has a good message, and it is so true! If you spread a little sugar, you most often get sugar right back. Of course, if you spread vinegar, you will get that right back too.

During the five-day inpatient stays for chemotherapy, one of two things could happen: either stay in my room and lament my circumstances or accept I was where I needed to be, getting the best care available, and make the most of it. I decided to be active, engaged, and positive. This attitude wasn't always easy to maintain, but it was necessary for my own well-being. The days were terribly long and awfully boring, so I did little things to make the day more pleasant. In turn, I found myself happier, which helped my mind and spirit set my body up in the best possible way to heal physically.

Random Acts of Kindness

Kindness affects the body and mind; there is scientific research behind it. Being kind stimulates the production of several chemicals in the brain, which is known as DOSE: dopamine, oxytocin, serotonin, and endorphins. These are what some call "feel-good chemicals" that can reduce anxiety, promote a positive outlook, and encourage a calm mood. For me, the more often I give kindness to others, the more this good feeling naturally occurs.

During those inpatient stays, the staff became an extended part of my family. The nurses and PCAs were so kind, often making me feel as if I was their only patient. They were my protectors, watching out for me and making sure to treat me as a person and not a number. They made all their patients feel special.

When arriving on Mondays for my five-day stay, the nurse would have a reflexology treatment and Urban Zen Reiki meditation session scheduled for me. Nurses brought me eye pillows, neck warmers, crochet caps, and various other fun little pampering gifts that were donated to the floor. These simple acts of kindness meant so much more to me than they will ever know. These little extras provided a needed distraction and sense of comfort at a time when I was scared and enveloped in fear. Those wonderful people made me laugh and feel normal and like someone who mattered. Princess Diana once said: "Carry out a random act of kindness with no expectation of reward, safe in the knowledge that one day someone might do the same for you."

Making Connections

One act of kindness can start a chain reaction. On my very first overnight stay at the James, John and I had to have looked like a couple of deer in the headlights when a patient approached us. She was also receiving inpatient chemotherapy, and she proceeded to welcome us and give us an orientation to the floor we were on. We talked all evening. She and her husband even shared some pizza they had ordered. We talked about her cancer journey and the success she was having with her treatments. Her story resonated with me, and I clung to her successful progress, which gave me hope.

On the Fourth of July, my family and many other members of the "Sixteenth-Floor Chemo Club" watched Columbus's huge "Red, White, and Boom" fireworks together. We all met on the fourteenth floor outdoor patio and enjoyed the show just a few miles away in downtown Columbus. Our families celebrated after with pizza and ice cream. This was one way we were able to turn a lousy situation into something positive, and that will always be a special memory. When life gave us lemons, we made a little lemonade and had a little sugar too.

Spreading Sugar of My Own

Trying to maintain my zeal for life was important, and so was inspiring that zeal in others. I don't want to come off as the cheerleader of the lymphoma floor just because I was out of my room interacting with others. Much of the reasoning was self-serving. Getting out of that room, not wallowing in self-pity, and spreading kindness to others helped to keep my mind in a positive place. Interactions with others lowered my anxiety and kept depression from overtaking my mind.

I'm a very strong believer that we attract what we put out. If I was going to focus on being sick and facing death, then that is what I would succumb to. Instead, being engaged with others filled me with hope. Positivity filled my heart and my very being, which made it easier to get rid of negative thoughts when they did creep in. Negativity was always lurking around my head and looking for a way in.

Staying positive took a lot of work. Some days were more successful than others, but no matter what, I kept trying. Being positive was key to my healing. We raise ourselves by lifting others through kindness.

Lessons Learned

1. When life gives you lemons, make lemonade. It is easier to mentally make a bad situation worse than to make it better. Showing kindness to others takes the emphasis off your own problems.
2. Spread a little love, and it will come back to you many times over. Kindness you receive from others can be wonderfully distracting from your own problems and can be the pick-me-up you need when feeling down.
3. A smile is just a frown turned upside down, but oh, what an impact it can have on everyone. It takes more muscles to frown than it does to smile. Quit working so hard!
4. You will reap what you sow. Plant some good seeds!

CHAPTER 5B: JOHN

Keep from Drowning!

Facing the worst

Early on in my teaching and coaching career, we lived in a very small town, and our school's volleyball team made it to the state finals. Sherri and I packed Nick, our only child at the time, in his car seat and headed down I-75 to Dayton, Ohio, and Wright State University. As we were rolling down the highway, we came up fast on a horrible accident. In fact, we, along with one other car, were the first ones on the scene. A minivan had veered off the highway near a bridge, apparently it had ridden right up the guardrail like a ramp, and careened through the air, landing on its roof. It was full of six members of a family.

When we came upon the vehicle, the bottom was smoking—and the wheels were still spinning. I was hesitant to get near the smoking vehicle, fearful it may explode. But Sherri? She just went to work like the veteran trauma nurse she was. The family was all unconscious. We had to get them out before the car went up in flames. Sherri was barking at everyone who had stopped to help. I fell in line like a soldier and did exactly what she said. When all six were out, she triaged them and found an elderly woman who was not breathing. Sherri went right to work doing CPR and brought her back. Once the authorities arrived, we gave a statement and left to continue on to the game. This memory is etched permanently in my brain. I will never forget it. I was literally shaking for quite a while after we left the scene. Sherri? She was on an adrenaline rush. Wow. She was amazing.

So, is it any wonder that when Sherri had to square off against cancer that she would be strong enough to face it head-on and conquer it? Nope! There is no doubt in my mind that her will to live and to beat this bastard is what carried her through all she endured. But this adversity was a whole different animal for me. Until my dad's passing, I truly never had to face the death—or even the potential death—of an immediate loved one. And adversity? The most adversity I ever had to deal with was the pressure to win football games during my twenty-three years as a head coach. And football was certainly not a life-and-death situation.

How do you face the potential long-term illness of a loved one or close friend as a caregiver? How do you one come to grips with the possible outcomes? How on earth do you keep from drowning? What does the future hold for us now? There was a chance Sherri might never work again and be forced to go on long-term disability. Our dreams of a long and productive retirement together would vanish. Worst of all, a voice in my head kept whispering, "This could take her life." Then what? This of course would take me down a whole new path of death preparations. My mind just churned endlessly and began creating the scenario where I would have to arrange a funeral and a burial. Worst of all was imagining having to say goodbye. My God, it rocked my world to contemplate all this.

Silence the Voices? No, But You Can Distract Them.

There was no choice. I had to step up to the plate and be there for Sherri. The next step was finding some way to quiet my own mind and stop listening to that voice of doubt and doom. But how do you silence your conscience? How do you tell your imagination to shut the hell up? While we were in the throes of treatments and recalling all the traumatic setbacks Sherri faced—and I witnessed—how could I possibly not be hearing those voices and thinking I might lose her? The key was to take the focus off what *might* happen to what was happening *now*. The thing is, I didn't even have to try. I had enough distractions to do it for me. You cannot downplay the power of the distractions that kept piling up. Maintaining my jobs (teaching and coaching), the travel to and from my two work locations to the hospital and home, the house, our finances and bills, dealing with insurance, tracking Sherri's appointments, continually questioning the doctors, researching all I could about the illness, the chemo, and meds, and just keeping our extended family updated provided me with tons of distractions and kept my mind in the present.

Providing Some Space

Having plenty to do myself was not a bad thing for Sherri either. While she was extremely happy to have me as a presence at the hospital and at home, some short times apart gave us some much-needed space. The last thing she wanted was me sitting and staring at her all day while she sat on the couch or napped.

Caregivers, some sage advice is to take time for yourself. The voices of worry and doom are not going anywhere, so taking some time for yourself is critical for your own mental and emotional health. It will help keep you on your A game. Your loved one depends on it. I knew if I was not in the right state of mind, I might miss an important instruction from the doctor, or worse, not notice something going on with Sherri. Whenever possible, I hit the gym and got in a workout a few times a week. This was a distraction of intent to force me to do something not related to cancer and caregiving. The hospital staff made it possible for me to workout at OSU's student rec center, which was a welcome blessing while Sherri was in treatment.

When the Voices Start Shouting

No, I could not always silence the voices. Sometimes, a situation just presents itself—and the voices start out loud and long. Like the day the official diagnosis came down and the C-word was dropped.

Everyone has these voices. We all have moments where we imagine a different life for ourselves. And by different, I don't mean better. So, let's give these voices a name: the "what-ifs." The "what-ifs" are our imaginations running wild.

Sherri had, and still has, a permanent case of the "what-ifs." Not a day goes by where a cough or a tightness in her chest doesn't start the voices chattering at her: "What if the lymphoma is back?" It only stands to reason that a caregiver will experience this too. Imaginations deal in the unknown, the unanticipated highs and lows of life.

Silencing the voices may be damn near impossible. First, accept them for what they are: a natural reaction to the vast collection of experiences, setbacks, and complications. Deal with them when you can by debunking those fears with facts. You can get the facts from professionals. Embrace the reality of the current situation. In other words, help your loved one understand that despite all these fears, they are simply not happening now. But when you cannot debunk them, by all means, distract the hell out of them as often as possible. Keep them busy and occupied with activity, a movie, or whatever else you can do.

"Is There Something We Can Do to Help?"

When Sherri got sick, I naturally took charge. Things were going to be done a certain way. Sherri was removed from all the decisions we always shared so she could focus on fighting the cancer and healing. By taking over literally everything, I certainly created a lot of stress for myself, but it was nothing compared to what Sherri was dealing with.

When people offered to help, I generally turned them down because things would not be done my way. I tend to be a bit of a perfectionist. Down the road, that would play itself out to the point where the offers stopped coming. Shame on me. I could have used the help for sure. But the flip side of that is sometimes I didn't really know what I needed. Many times, when someone tries to help, it creates more work because you have to show them how to do something repeatedly when it would be easier to do it yourself! Yes, I could have used some help. If the offers had been directed at something specific, that would have worked. The bottom line is that asking for and receiving help is a great way to be a more effective caregiver. To maximize this, both those who wish to help and caregivers can really make it work with some simple guidelines.

Takeaways

1. Caregivers need help too. "Me" time may be impossible as some caregivers are alone; it is just the patient and the caregiver. Others have entire families around to chip in and help take care of little ones, aging parents, etc. Let me offer some advice to both caregivers and to those who may be reading this that have offered to help someone in need:

   a. Do not be afraid of asking for help or accepting it.

   b. Give people credit that they are capable and smart and can be of real assistance.

   c. Be specific and ask for what you need. Need some help watching the kids or running them around? You know at least one person who probably could help. Need help with meal prep or shopping? Or maybe just a chance to get away for a couple hours? I am sure you can find at least one person who could assist.

d. It's simple: people on the outside looking in don't know what you need, so speak up and tell them.

e. If you are far away from home in an extended stay with your loved one, you need time for yourself. Talk with the hospital staff about some options you might enjoy. It will help you reset for the next battle.

2. For any readers who just want to help because you care about someone:

a. Be clear and offer a specific way you know you can help.

b. Maybe your friends' contributions will be to make runs to the store. Even helping make the list and place the order for home delivery would be awesome.

c. If there are children in the mix, take them to a movie or something! I would have loved to have someone actually call up and offer something very specific they could do for us because sometimes I didn't know what help I really needed.

d. Another suggestion is to narrow it down to the date and time you will offer to help. Caregivers like me are stubborn and will push you off, thinking we can handle things. Specifying a date and time ensures it will happen. And you caregivers don't be stubborn! Lean on those who want to help—just tell them precisely what you need. Specify dates and times. It matters!

3. We owe so much to so many. While we can never repay our gratitude, Sherri being able to live a full life and simply be here every day is the reward of everyone's efforts—from the hospital team right down to Sherri herself and her will to win.

CHAPTER 6A: SHERRI

The Good. The Bad. The Ugly

Surprising Issues with the Healthy World

The good, the bad, the ugly isn't the Clint Eastwood motion picture I am talking about; these are the file into which anyone who is sick, suffering or recovering can categorize all of the family, friends, coworkers, acquaintances, and just general well-wishers. People—even with all the best intentions to mean well—can often cause more harm than good. Still others hit a proverbial home run in offering support and help. My hope is that perhaps what is shared here will serve as an example of what to do and what not to do when offering support. Read on!

The *Really* Good

Before we discuss the good, let's talk about the really, *really* good. You cannot overstate that support is so important to healing. Mentally, having a strong support system can provide a huge lift when you are feeling down, scared, or overwhelmed. I had support teams in two places: one at the hospital and of course one at home. In the hospital, the nurses, PCAs, nurse practitioners, and doctors were all a part of a vast network of support. Even the custodial and food service employees were part of my team, offering a kind smile or conversation.

The hospital team physically administered medications, changed dressings, helped empty colostomy bags, and even helped me walk. They held the bucket and rubbed my back while vomiting, and they helped me shower or take a dry bath when beyond my capability. Through all that, they also found a way to help me smile and even laugh when things most definitely were not laughable. There were times when I was feeling distraught, but then one of those wonderful people would drop a one-liner that would make us all laugh. When I first had a colostomy bag, and it was leaking poop all down my stomach (so gross), someone said, "Well, aren't you just a party pooper!" Those were the moments in time I will always remember because a kind or funny word provided a much-needed boost to my mental and emotional state. And that was just the hospital part of my support team.

My Home Team Was Undeniably Incredible.

I was very fortunate to have wonderful caregivers throughout my illness and beyond. Some people have no one. Still others would be better off not having a caregiver at all. Now this may sound shocking, but if the caregiver cannot handle giving up their own needs and being thrown into a role they never asked for, imagine how toxic that situation could be! A patient battling for their life needs an incredible amount of help and patience. All their energy and focus must be focused on themselves and healing. On the flip side of that, it takes an incredibly special person to be a caregiver because they must give of themselves unconditionally. Often, caregivers get nothing in return except having to deal with a patient who rides a roller coaster of moodiness, nausea, vomiting, and fatigue. Caregivers will spend their time literally managing the household, finances, and chores—often alone.

John was with me every step of the way. There is simply no way to ever thank him for all he did. Our three boys were young adults who were just starting their professional lives. The oldest of our boys, Nick, was serving in the army and was stationed overseas in Germany. Then we have the twins. Beau graduated from the Ohio State University and had just landed his first job several states away. Brian was living at home and working in a research lab at OSU while busy applying to medical school; he was a big help to John and me. One thing I made emphatically clear was there was no way I would allow my cancer diagnosis to get in the way of their plans or careers! Nick and Beau were always calling and checking in since they could not be here physically.

The Three Amigos!

My parents are retired and do what a lot of other retirees do: take little jaunts and stay continually active. So, when we made the call for help, they answered. We were so very fortunate they could stay with us during the week, Monday through Friday, so John was able to continue working. John was still managing our affairs along with preparing and teaching his students and coaching football. Bev and Bill could pick up the slack and help manage me. They were a shoulder to cry on when I needed to sob, and they provided laughter to lighten a mood (sometimes on purpose and other times just by being them). My parents were never pushy or intrusive; they were just there to lend a hand and lighten the load. No matter how old we get, in our parents' eyes, we are always their children. Even though I was fifty years old, clearly, I still needed Mom and Dad!

They would load me up in the car, and we would take long sightseeing drives, go to parks for a walk, or even take in a movie. What a team we were! These little jaunts were often the highlight of my day, and they served as a way to escape my world for a bit. Those escapes were so precious, and they will always remain cherished memories.

We used to laugh a lot. One day, we started calling ourselves the "three amigos." In the evenings, John would come home worried about me and want to ask me how I did through the day. He would often find us talking and giggling about what we did that day, the day he wasn't a part of. It was like we had our own little club, and he wasn't a member. John had to shoulder a very heavy load, and he didn't get to experience any of the lightheartedness my parents tried to supply. Looking back, I feel a little selfish now; it just wasn't on my radar that he might be struggling.

The Good

Good friends are sometimes few and far between in this life. Good friends are the ones you know will be there when times get really tough. They call or stop by to see how you are or if your family needs anything. Maybe most importantly, they still treat you as "you." The "good" were friends who stopped by just to talk and treated me like I was still the same person.

Two of my closest friends from work brought a basket of gag gifts that had absolutely *nothing* to do with being sick. We laughed, and they filled me in on all the gossip I was missing at work. We laughed so hard that my side started to hurt. In those moments, if only for a moment, I forgot about cancer. These were the absolute best visits: visits from people who just came to say hello with no expectations of how they thought I would be. They were not tiptoeing around on eggshells, worried they might say the wrong thing. They didn't sneak weird glimpses at me and my bald head. They just came to hang out and bring joy to my heart.

The "good" were also those friends who rolled up their sleeves and chipped in. Nick's in-laws, who are close friends, were there for John and me any time of day or night. They would bring meals to the house or sit with us at the hospital. I knew I could count on them for anything—and so could John. They would quietly check in and anticipate needs we may have before we even thought of it. They would drop off meals or a gift card for John for gas or mail a funny note in a card. All these little things matter—trust me.

Keeping my attitude positive was a huge challenge for me and for John. Some friends assumed the role of being my pep coaches. One close friend decided that was the role for her. She came to visit and just lit up the room with positivity. On one occasion, she had made a special wall hanging with small clips. Along with that was a box that was full of positive motivational messages. I would pick out the message cards that "spoke to me" that day and clip them to the wall hanging where I could see them when I needed a lift. Additionally, she would send me a daily "thinking of you" text, which I looked forward to.

Many other visitors would call and ask if it was OK to stop by. These visitors stayed just long enough to show they cared and left, knowing a short visit was all I needed or could withstand. These visits are so positive toward healing. And of course, all the meals and thoughtful gifts that so many others provided will last in my memory and were a huge part of my recovery. Knowing people love you and care is as energizing and healing as any medication will ever be. They feed the soul and lift the spirit.

The Bad

The "bad" may be an unfair moniker because many of the good people in this category, although their actions were awkward and uncomfortable, had their hearts in the right place. These folks just don't know how to handle being around someone who is sick. This has been written with the sincerest of intentions; there is a right way and a wrong way to show support for those you care about.

The Checklist Bunch

Experience is the greatest teacher, so here are a few examples of "the bad" to illustrate what I mean. One day, I had a visitor who I barely know as an acquaintance. She stopped by to visit, and she brought her husband with her. I had never met him and this visit was unannounced. They stayed and visited for more than an hour. She began talking and talking about her adult kids; I didn't even know she had any, but it seemed like she had a hundred children—plus all the grandkids. My mind was not even thinking clearly enough to grasp the Ancestry.com version of this couple's family. Making matters worse, being completely bald, I thought, *Hey, thanks for showing up without a warning and for bringing your husband since I'm looking my best and have never even met him!*

We call these the "check it off my list" people. These visitors really may have had good intentions, but they were out to satisfy their own needs. One need was their curiosity; they wanted to get "the scoop" as to what was happening with me so they could go back and share it with everyone they know who might know of me. *Oh, the poor thing. No, she is not looking good. Not good at all. Oh, yes, we both really enjoyed the visit!* I can just imagine the lunchroom talk.

A better option before you go visit someone you know is sick, exhausted, and immunocompromised is to call first to see if visiting is OK. Another need these visitors have is the need for recognition. Some just feel the need to be recognized by everyone as being kindhearted and letting everyone know they reached out and visited. I call it "look at me" syndrome. I'm not saying this was in their conscious mind when they visited; their hearts were in a good place, but bragging rights were definitely tangible benefits. Now they could let the world know what was going on, and everyone in their circles would know how wonderful they are because they took the time to visit.

The "Living My Best Life" Brigade

Then there were the visitors who came to see me who thought their one purpose in stopping by was to share all the great things happening in their lives. Now, I want to word this carefully because I would absolutely never wish a terrible illness on anyone. No, I didn't want to be seen as the pitiful "woe is me" cancer patient. And, yes, of course I did like visits that didn't talk about me and being ill. But there should definitely be some sensitivity etiquette when talking about what's going on in the real world and sharing all about your "once-in-a-lifetime trip" you are leaving for or perhaps just returned from. Or that you are going to the "best concert ever" followed by "the greatest party" ever. I do want to hear about your good fortune and fun times. However, sharing every detail, every photo, every it was "the best time ever" is hard to swallow when you are on house arrest or bedridden. Yes, I'm glad you are living life, but it can feel like someone rubbing salt in a wound. It just did not occur to these visitors that maybe I would never be able to enjoy these things in life again. *Don't they see that I am in a battle for my life and that, God forbid, my days may be numbered? Have some empathy, people!*

Oh, Look! They Brought the Kids!

Besides knowing not to show up without calling first, do not compound that situation by towing your kids along into an immunocompromised home. Having children around can bring a lot of joy, but kids also bring germs in the form of runny, snotty noses and uncovered coughing, and they touch everything. Many people often feel that since "my kids aren't sick," it is OK to bring them into any environment and save the hassle of finding a sitter. They just do not think this through, and in their earnest attempt to check in and visit, they can easily expose someone with a compromised immune system to a cold, the flu, or other viruses. This is a recipe for potentially dangerous complications and delays in treatment or recovery. Being around the enthusiasm and innocent happiness of youth can be healing for sure. The bottom line for visitors is to be kind and simply ask to make sure the patient is comfortable with children tagging along.

The Ugly

Now we pay tribute to those who simply do not understand any rules of etiquette. Whether it was a call or a physical visit, these well-wishers would leave me literally in tears and feeling like I ought to just chuck it all and go pick out a casket. These people are similar to the folks who tell pregnant women about the worst birth or pregnancy stories that have ever happened, leaving an excited, soon-to-be mom in a state of panic and unease. Yes, you know who these people are. These are the people who, no matter what happens to you, it happened to them ten times worse. It's not like they are trying to keep up with the Joneses. No, it's much worse: they want to beat the crap out of the Joneses and make them look inconsequential. So, here we go. Let's talk about some examples.

Ugly

I will start with the "grim reapers" calling when they hear about a cancer diagnosis. Now they may call or visit to check in, but inevitably, they begin spreading misery. A "cheery" grim reaper called to see how I was doing, but within minutes, they proceeded to tell me how everyone around them was dead from cancer and the many gruesome complications those people suffered. Why would anyone say this to someone with a potentially terminal condition? Unfortunately, there were many incidents of insensitive people who didn't think before they spoke, leaving me speechless and dumbfounded. For my own self-preservation, I stopped taking calls from people like that and avoided them in social situations. Even though it may cause hurt feelings to these "well-wishers," I had to ignore them for my own well-being.

Even Uglier

There are several subcategories to this grouping, and they all have uniquely irritating characteristics

The Whispering Pity-Party Bunch

It was inevitable. Everywhere I went, someone would discreetly let all the people around know how I had just undergone cancer treatments. Whisper, whisper, whisper. This group, with their not-so-subtle stares, glances, and whispers, made me feel like I had two heads growing out of my neck. I just wanted to be another regular person. I'm just Sherri and not the "cancer girl." Let me blend in with everyone else.

Some people will never see me as anything but the cancer girl. They are the ones who approach me slowly, almost cautiously, as if they are walking on eggshells. They tilt their heads the way they do when expressing condolences at a funeral home, soften their eyes, and quiet their voice, gently asking, "So, how are you doing?" They ask it as if expecting a response like, "Well, thanks so much for asking. The cancer is back, and I'm a goner." If it happens to be in a group setting, I get singled out with this pitiful greeting while everyone else gets an energetic "Hi! How's it going?" Please don't be that person.

"I Wanna Talk about Me" Bunch

Once I became active and was back out in public and at work, it was inevitable this would happen. Being in health care probably increases the likelihood that someone will approach me and congratulate me on beating cancer—but then they unload a litany of personal problems. One incident stands out. This person happens to have irritable bowel syndrome, fibromyalgia, asthma, and whatever other malady you can think of. If you bring it up, they either had it, have it, or are going to get it. And, when they do get it, it will be worse than anyone else has ever experienced. One day they saw me and told me how great it was to see me because "I had no one to talk to about my irritable bowel issues and how gassy and bloated I have been for the past year." I mean, holy shit! I just missed almost an entire year of my life from cancer, and this is what they say to me? I said, "I don't know how I could be so selfish and not be there to hear about your gas problems." Pretty subtle, right? My sarcasm went right over their head. People like that cannot see past their noses—so just let them talk, but don't take on their baggage.

The Experts

Then you have the people who know someone else with the disease "XYZ," the same thing you have. And this, of course, makes them an expert. Every time I saw this one individual, I got a play-by-play of a family member's case of lymphoma. Yes, you guessed it, things didn't go very well, and he ultimately died from it. I heard this story more than once. Even now, when the individual sees me coming, the question I get is (brace yourself), "When do they expect your lymphoma to come back? It always does." I just want to scream. How can people be so blind to their own words? I avoid that person to this very day.

Lessons Learned

Advice for Visitors and Well-Wishers

1. Abide by the golden rule, and if you can't say something nice, don't say anything at all. Unless you have been through something similar, you don't get it. And that's OK. It is fine if you don't know what to say. Unfortunately, your words are not going to make everything OK anyway—so quit worrying about it. This is a journey that must be taken and completed by the patient, but you can take the journey alongside them. Just being there is enough.

2. Like Samwise in *The Lord of the Rings*—forgive me if you don't know the story, but it was a house favorite for our sons growing up—says when Frodo must carry an evil ring to be destroyed: "I can't carry the ring for you, but I can carry you!" A friend can be there in so many other ways by lending an ear, being a shoulder to cry on, or just giving a hug.

3. As a nurse who works with people when they are going through devastating and traumatic times, I always thought I really had the right thing to say at just the right moment. Looking back after having been on the patient side of things, I realize I don't have to have the perfect quote—and I am not going to make things better. However, I can offer genuine kindness and a listening ear. I have a good friend who always seems to know what to say, and I even enjoy watching her engage in conversation with others. She once told me a quote she tries to live by: "Listen to understand not to react." Don't think about what you want to say or need to say; instead, react to what is actually being said to you. This is what I try to do, and that is what you can do too when offering support.

4. Don't tell death stories or horror stories about people you know who went through hell. Just don't. I am trying to recover and am still living in the shadow of the illness. It's rotten, selfish, and just plain stupid. Stories like these serve no purpose, and they only create fear and anxiety for the patient. Frankly, doing so could probably be labeled as some form of verbal abuse for all the damage it can do.

5. Prearrange everything. Coordinate all visits, gifts, and food through the caregiver. Always check to see if what you want to do is appropriate. Ask what is needed, or better yet, offer some ideas to the caregiver about what you could do to help. If the patient is close to a family with children, they may like a visit with the kids. Just check in advance to see if it is OK.

6. Don't visit for long, and by all means, don't bring more germs into the patient's environment. Remember, having compassion requires courtesy. Being courteous is showing compassion. Wear a mask, use hand sanitizer, and respect social distancing. Don't visit if you are feeling ill.

7. Thoughtful trinkets, small meaningful gifts, cards, and messages are all so welcome. When I was bald and losing weight, a warm hat and scarf were the best gifts ever.

8. Do your best to be empathetic. Think before you act. Try to walk in the patient's shoes, and maybe, just maybe, you will be amazing at being supportive.

My Fellow Warriors

1. Just be blunt and direct with people. If you have had enough, tell them it is time to leave. In the end, you'll both be happier that you were direct. I should have been more forthright with people. Just like with caregivers, forget the manners. You can say you're sorry later. Battling, healing, and recovering come first.

2. It's hard, but do not be afraid to tell people they are hurting you more than helping. Some people simply don't know what they cannot see—and so many are blind to their own actions and language. Speak up and point it out to them. This goes back to being direct. They don't know what they don't know.

CHAPTER 6B: JOHN

Being a People Filter

The Problem with People

A filter is designed to remove impurities and generally "bad stuff" from a substance to make it safe for us to use or consume. So, who would think that a person would need a "human filter" to protect them from other well-meaning people? Sounds absolutely crazy to say it aloud. Yet inevitably, one of my major roles as a caregiver was to become a protective filter for Sherri. I was sort of like a buffer between the healthy world and Sherri's world of treatment and recovery. I became a shield of defense from people who, though well-meaning, might inundate her with messages, calls, and visits—or even viruses and bugs that could compromise her health altogether. They could cause her great duress and anxiety, which would certainly prevent or delay the healing process.

We Just Want to Help

When bad things happen, people really do want to help. The world is full of individuals who, to their very core, are wonderful, caring, and compassionate. But at the same time, when you or a loved one are struck with illness, you can expect a full-blown dose of both kindness and downright awkwardness from people who want to provide support.

Imagine, as a caregiver, trying to navigate through this labyrinth of diagnosis, treatment, and recovery while having to teach people the right way to help. For me, sometimes it was fielding and fending off phone calls by saying, "I'll call you when I have news to share; otherwise, don't expect me to constantly update you." Other times, I had to be the bad guy and literally tell some people to limit all the calls and texts.

Before the official diagnosis, we really did not let anyone know what was going on with Sherri's health other than her parents and our sons. For all we knew, Sherri just had a nasty infection like bronchitis. At that time, it was clear that alerting our two families and all of our friends would only create confusion and curiosity. It was not until she was diagnosed that I needed a method of informing everyone.

My Mom: The Informant

Diagnosis: Cancer! The news came like a ton of bricks. Once the news dropped, and I assumed the "rank" of caregiver, one of my first duties was notifying family and friends. Sherri, the newly diagnosed patient, was way too distraught with grief and worry to start calling people. What would that be like? "Hey, there—guess what! I've got cancer!" Frankly, who wants to make a couple dozen phone calls and have to explain the situation over and over. Nightmare for sure! I quickly found a solution.

My dear mother! If it needs to be told, she is the one to do it. She can get information out to the family in a matter of minutes. In fact, she and I kid about this all the time. Anytime she calls, I know the first thing she will utter are the latest obituaries from home. If it happened to be anyone she knew or thought I knew, she is going to give me the full report.

Knowing that Mom is the ultimate champion informant, I decided to take full advantage of her skill set. I was able to fill her in with the whole story about Sherri's biopsy and that she had a rare lymphoma. So, I called Mom and unloaded the awful news. I explained every detail that we did know, and I commissioned her to perform the task of notifying all the rest of the Snoad family, including aunts and uncles. My mom was to become an informant.

The last instructions were a clear message to convey to all my siblings: "Please don't call me right now. Just wait. I will be texting out information to the group as I learn it. Please don't bombard Sherri. She was still trying to process the news and wrap her head around the uncertain future of her very life."

The process was repeated with Sherri's parents, but Sherri was part of that conference call. Sherri has a smaller family, and talking to her parents was pretty therapeutic and just plain good for her. Having a simplified way to notify everyone would make my life a lot easier.

Letting family, friends, and work associates know what was going on was no treat. The repetitive calls and rehashing the entire story were brutal and exhausting, particularly on my emotions.

Enough Already!

I had to act. There just was no choice. Though I regret how it was done without her consent, I decided to tell everyone in Sherri's phonebook to not text her and to go through me using my phone number. At the time, it seemed like the right decision. Watching her get flustered and driven to tears as people would not leave her alone was exasperating. Many people cannot end a text conversation and feel like they always have to respond. Sherri never knew when to politely end a text conversation. She has some really great, well-meaning friends, but they had no idea what her condition was—and she was still trying to understand what it all meant. We would be sitting at home or in the hospital room, and that phone of hers would be blowing up with alerts.

For the first couple of weeks after her treatments began, she was spending an inordinate amount of time trying to respond to people. She was growing more exhausted and frustrated, and she just wanted to chuck her phone. I began forming a plan. After we came home from her first round of treatments, the fatigue set in, and she wanted to sleep much of the time.

After running some errands on the first day home from treatment, I came home to find her sound asleep. Her phone was busy flashing notifications. I did it while she was asleep. Sherri had been crying about all the texts and not wanting to upset people by not responding, and I could not stand seeing that beat her down. Taking her phone, I sat down in the easy chair and, unbeknownst to her, prepared a message. I sent it to literally everyone in her phone book who I knew was texting her. My message was not harsh or unkind, and it expressed to all what she was experiencing and the great stress she was under feeling compelled to respond to all and carry on lengthy chats. I gave them my number and asked that they text me for information and updates—but only every couple of weeks or so. I mentioned that if Sherri reached out to them, it was fine to reply. My last instruction was to not respond to this mass message. What a nightmare if she were to wake up to a dozen more text messages responding to the one I sent! The plan was to not tell Sherri right away. *Mistake!*

All calls and messages to Sherri stopped. She was so upset and thought no one cared because they weren't contacting her anymore. I had to confess what I did. My plan backfired. Sherri was extremely upset with me for secretly cutting off all the messages. She was more hurt than anything. While she appreciated the thought behind it and the pressure it relieved, she had every right to be upset with me. I do not regret doing the deed. My regret lies in not having a serious discussion with her about it first. Instead, I acted impulsively.

Bridge the Gap

The things I wish I had known going into all this are numerous. While I am tech-savvy when it comes to production tools on a computer, my social media knowledge at that time was miniscule. Social media was a foreign language until I joined Facebook the same year as Sherri's cancer diagnosis. Heck, I only did it to follow and get ticket information on my new favorite music group.

Perhaps if I was more tech-savvy at that time, I would have discovered that there were online sites where a person can create a communication journal and invite friends and family to join it. The caregiver—or someone else on their behalf—can post updates about the patient. A journal would have allowed all these caring people—family, friends, and coworkers—to post comments and well-wishes in a common place. Sherri would have been able to log in at her leisure and read or respond whenever she wanted. No inundating text messages to stress her anymore.

It is a bit baffling that someone in support services did not mention this idea, but in the end, I should have done some homework myself. We came across one particular online blog that really bridges that gap between patients and their loved ones and friends when a coworker at one of Sherri's schools was diagnosed with cancer. This was over a year after Sherri was released from treatments. We both went on and left kind and encouraging messages for this person. We were amazed by the site and how much we would have used it!

People and Their Peculiar Behaviors

The day the doctor told us Sherri was cured and the chemo was no longer needed was a day we took a deep breath and let out a major sigh of relief. And at the same time, we both asked that proverbial question: "Now what?" The twisted roads to recovery are bad enough. Trying to figure out how to get some sense of normalcy back *and* overcoming all the complications that had ravaged Sherri's body gave both of us all we could handle. Let's throw another variable into all of this chaotic uncertainty: people and their peculiar ways of showing they are sympathetic to the situation and wanting to be compassionate. Read on.

Please Do Not Say That to Her

Once we announced to basically everyone in our world that Sherri had beaten this thing called cancer, you would think they would want to move on with us. Not so fast. What we quickly discovered is that some people now identified Sherri as the "cancer girl" and it is *still* an issue for some.

I love clever anecdotes and motivational sayings, especially those that provide guidance and inspiration. One that has resounded with me over the years is this: "Don't let your past define you." I don't know where it originated, but it is fitting. It is hard enough to change your own way of thinking and break free of the crippling chains of past events or mistakes in your life. For some, it is too much to overcome. All I know is that my wife, my warrior, was beyond ready to be done with cancer, and she certainly did not want it to define her. During treatment, Sherri made every effort to combat the image of being known as a cancer patient. For example, she never wore hospital gowns or lounged around in pajamas and a robe at home. She dressed herself every day in her athletic running gear and made sure the world saw her as "Sherri" and not someone with a potentially terminal illness. She got up out of her hospital bed and sat in a chair, walked the halls, and fought to keep her self-image one of empowerment. When declared a survivor, that was not enough for Sherri. Nope. Victorious was what she felt. She felt like a conqueror and was ready to seize life and truly live again. Then why couldn't others join her in seeing this perspective instead of defining her as a cancer victim?

Sherri got so fed up with the looks of pity and people continually asking her how she was doing. They also would quietly ask me the same things. They might pull me aside to pitifully ask how she was doing.

It is such a fine line with this scenario. Certainly, it is great that people care enough to express concern and ask how she is doing. She has been free of cancer for some time, but people still do the pitiful head tilt thing. So, my newest strategy is to head it off. When people ask me that same question with that same pathetic tone and tilt, I look at them and say, "Aw, thanks so much for asking, but she is doing just fine. In fact, when you see her, she would much rather just be treated like someone who never had cancer." Instead of asking how she is feeling or doing, she would prefer to be asked what she has been up to lately, about work or our kids—or, hell, about anything else. Just please don't pour on the concern and condolence-like pity! Yes, I have had to train people to move on. She certainly has—why can't everyone else?

The Impossibles

Being a buffer for Sherri was not always easy. There were times at school or football when I was simply not able to curtail some of the visits. What I observed as a result of these unwelcome visits in terms of Sherri's reactions was disturbing and infuriating. Clearly, some people do not know the mental anguish that can be caused by the wrong words. For example, we had one set of well-wishers who I refer to as "The Impossibles." I cannot overstate the amount of grief they caused. Eventually, they served to alter Sherri's behavior.

The Impossibles showed up to our home unannounced on a few separate occasions, but I was only there for one of them. Sure, they had good intentions in visiting. I keep telling myself that anyway—as I shake my head and wonder how they could not have known what they were doing to her.

The first couple of visits, which occurred during treatment, started out nicely enough, but by the time they left, Sherri felt as if she should call the funeral home, order the casket, and throw in the towel. The conversations they had with her centered around having no control, that cancer is a killer, and maybe she should just accept the fact that eventually, it will take her life. Yes, they really said that. I cannot begin to explain to you how grief-stricken she was when she told me about their visits. They really got into her head, and I had to talk her off the edge of the cliff each time.

Not by chance, they were in the neighborhood and decided to pop in again without warning, and this time, Sherri was in full recovery. When the doorbell rang, she froze. She was always on the alert for them. When she got a glimpse through the door glass, she bolted from the room. That was the last time I would see Sherri for an hour. I kept the Impossibles out of the house, and they finally left. When they arrived, she had bolted from our home, unbeknownst to me, to escape seeing them. I could not locate Sherri. I was walking all through the house, yelling for her, and looking everywhere. She had developed a real fear of being dragged into an abyss of their misery that would become her reality.

That is the effect that people can have, often unknowingly, on someone who is physically, mentally, and emotionally compromised. They already are living in fear of the illness, the possible outcome, or the chances of it returning. As a caregiver, you *must* be ready to act. As a potential well-wisher, think about what you do and say *before* you do or say anything!

It took me an hour to find her. The neighbor rang the doorbell and let me know Sherri was next door. He asked if I needed any help getting rid of the Impossibles; apparently, Sherri had told him the whole story.

Takeaways

1. Just do your thing as a caregiver should. Intervene and get out in front of everything. You can avoid a lot of bad situations by being proactive and expecting the unexpected

2. Have a plan, even for unannounced or unwelcome visits. I do wish we had been better prepared and more outspoken during some of those bad experiences. Feelings and politeness be damned; your loved one's health and welfare are all that matters.

3. Be blunt. Be honest and give it to 'em straight. Egos will recover. Have no fear in saying no or telling someone it is time to leave. Do not feel guilt for protecting your loved one. You might have to teach others how to act, what to say, and when to say it. The first time is the toughest. After that, you will have no trouble telling people like it is.

4. Take advantage of modern technology to create a private and manageable social media outlet for all parties involved. If texts and calls get overwhelming, then limit communication—but be sure to make those decisions *with* your loved one. It was not just my decision to make.

5. Be able to laugh at some of the crazy things people say and do. At the time, it may not seem funny, but laugh at it and let it go. Nothing is permanent.

CHAPTER 7A: SHERRI

Do You Remember the Time …?

Dealing with Chemo Brain

Read all you want about "chemo brain." The internet can provide all sorts of articles, and the experts have given it many names: chemo brain, chemo fog, cancer-related cognitive impairment, or cognitive dysfunction. You can call it whatever you want. It just plain sucks! A lot of the articles simply explained the effects of chemotherapy, but they do not at all get into why concentration and memory issues are the norm after cancer treatments. There are whole checklists of side effects, and I can check off every one of them.

- Unusually disorganized: check
- Difficulty finding the right word or words: check.
- Difficulty multitasking: check. I try, but I'm all over the place and easily distracted.
- Short-term memory problems: check. Um, where did I park?
- Trouble with verbal memory: check. Such as remembering a conversation.
- Mental fogginess: check. Like much of the time!

While you may have heard of chemo brain and wondered if it really is a thing, well, it is. If you have it or had it (for me, I think it is going to be a forever thing), then you already know how frustrating it is. I still have difficulty recalling simple things that happened the day before. At times, my lack of short-term recall downright scares me. Fear preys on me, and worry sets in that I may have dementia or am experiencing the onset of Alzheimer's disease. How must I seem to those around me?

Speaking in groups or at meetings was something I used to embrace and enjoy, but now I dread it. The thought of public speaking petrifies me. Intelligent words or thoughts either escape me or get stuck and swirl around in my head. Sometimes what comes out is simply way off base from my original intention.

My problem-solving skills often seemed a step behind, especially during the entire first year after chemo. As a nurse, thinking and reacting to crises on the spot came natural to me before chemo. Problem-solving once was a talent. I effectively used as few steps as possible to complete a task efficiently. Now my thought processes take me down a path of needless, cumbersome steps to get the task done. I must think through how I am going to complete everything. There are so many gaps in my thought processes to overcome.

My Life as an Etch-a-Sketch!

Do you remember what an Etch-a-Sketch is? Possibly you had one when you were a child. The user creates a picture on a screen using two dials. It is full of aluminum powder that sticks to the screen. The dials move a pointed stylus inside the screen, creating whatever image you want. The tricky part is working both dials at the same time and making the pencillike stylus draw your image. One dial makes horizontal lines, and the other makes vertical ones. If you want anything other than straight lines, your two hands must work in tandem to get curves, turns or diagonals. The skill required to make precise drawings is incredible. It takes practice to master the device.

The long-term effects of chemo caused me to feel as if my mind was an Etch-a-Sketch, but with the hands of two different people—each on a dial competing to create their own image! Literally, the right hand didn't know what the left hand was doing. As a result, the lines produced look more like a random doodle without organization or cohesiveness. That is what goes on in my head. Point A and point B are visible, but the path to connect them is a maze.

If you just pick it up and shake, you will have a fresh blank screen, wiping out anything you just did. Hello, short-term memory loss! It was as if my mind was constantly being shaken up, like pushing a reset button, and my ability to recall recent events was diminished. Truthfully, many events, conversations, and milestones that happened once chemo started have fallen victim to short-term memory loss. My one successful solution has been journaling so I can go back and recall the past.

Chemo Fog versus Chemo Brain

The experts may say "chemo fog" is just another name for "chemo brain," but in my experiences, they presented as two separate conditions. The "fog" of chemotherapy occurs and thickens when a plethora of medications are added to the treatment plan to coincide with it or offset side effects. These additional medications often carry their own side effects, which impact mental functioning. For me, chemo brain defines the aftereffects of treatment, which are a more permanent normal. Chemo brain is the long-term side effects and changes as a direct result of treatment, and it lingers for an indefinite period of time. It may never completely disappear.

There Is No Manual

"It just takes time," the doctors will tell you. "Oh, you'll be back to normal soon," they'll say. There is no one handing out manuals with a step-by-step formula for how to get your mind and life back. You don't suddenly wake up, read a how-to book, and feel like "you" again. Not by a long shot. I still am on this unbelievable journey to find "me," and though progress has been slow but steady, the journey goes on.

Face facts: cancer and chemo do change you. They changed me. For a long time, I did not recognize myself physically or mentally, but at least I can sleep a little easier at night knowing that the cause has a face and name. And there is an army of us; you are not alone. The research that exists supports the existence of chemo brain but is quite limited in specifying the long-term impact.

Who Moved My Car?

Everyone forgets where they parked the car occasionally. In fact, it is normal for many people to experience this lapse in short-term memory. When you head off to the grocery store or mall, some of them have signs to let you know what section you parked in. But after chemo, this experience was different—very different.

Stepping out of the store one day and glancing across the parking lot, everything went completely blank. There was a sea of cars; the lot didn't even look remotely familiar. I had no idea which direction to start walking. There was an instant of fear, which was actually more like terror and panic! Not wanting anyone to notice, I focused on remaining calm. Then out into the sea of automobiles I waded, taking my best guess at where I had parked.

At some point during my wandering, I realized I could use the alarm button on the key fob, but I would only use that as a last resort. Pride prevented me from hitting that button. Fortunately, I'm often not the only one wandering the parking lot jungle. Before too long, I had struck up a conversation with another wanderer, and we were roaming the parking lot together and looking for our lost vehicles. We tend to bond, my fellow wanderers and I, and as a team, we help each other out, only parting ways as we both find our vehicles. Which of course, is cause for celebration.

The "Paper Attacher Thingamajig"

Regardless of knowing what I want to say, my brain scrambles the words, and something totally different will spill out of my mouth. When looking for a bowl, I'll ask, "Could you hand me a cup?" In need of a glass, I might say plate. At least I am in the right category of kitchenware! After a recent snow, I asked John if he was going to mow the driveway! The inability to recall words, names, or objects is unpredictable, but it happens more frequently, like most of my issues, when my body and mind are fatigued.

My brain feels as if it has been split in two; part of it knows what I want to say, but the other part spews out the wrong words. When feeling excited or animated, the words jump around in my head and come out flowing as fast as Spaniards trying to outrun the bulls in Pamplona. But when the words leave my mouth to be spoken aloud, they come out as if the bulls have trampled them!

Consciously taking a different approach when the wrong word comes out has helped. I pause and search the labyrinth of my mind for the right word. Slowing down my brain helps and allows the correct word to find its way out. Pausing to think before speaking is not easy and requires practice and a lot of patience.

At work one day, looking to borrow a stapler, I asked a coworker if I could borrow hers. And here is how this simple request went: "Hey can I borrow your ..." My brain went totally blank. There was no way I could think of the word *stapler*. I proceeded to explain that I needed a "tool, you know, that keeps papers together permanently."

For the longest time, she looked at me and then said, "Do you mean my stapler?"

Throwing my hands up in the air, I shouted, "Yes! That's it!"

It was as frustrating and as it was comical. *Frustration* is a word I will *never* have trouble recalling because I feel frustrated so much of the time!

Huh?

Getting together with friends and families is good for the soul, but it also presents a few challenges. During the course of a conversation, people talk and laugh about past events and memories. Often due to the effects of chemotherapy, I find myself having no recollection of what is being talked about. I may not remember, but I laugh along and fake it pretty well by asking broad questions that help me narrow in and recall what they are talking about. "Fake it 'til you make it" as they say. Short-term memory recall was a serious issue for quite a while in recovery. Good news though; this has improved with time as well as my tricks to figure out the gist of a conversation so I can participate without anyone knowing.

Fitting a Square Peg into a Round Hole

Looking at the big picture? Multitasking? These aren't so easy anymore. The straight line to get me from point A to point B is now a curvy road with plenty of switchbacks. When working on projects and tasks that require multiple-step thought processing, I am not always able to see that big picture or the next steps that are needed to carry out the task. I may get sidetracked and move on to a different project, often coming up with that next step for the previous project while doing the new project!

Sometimes the answers appear minutes later—and sometimes the next day. Through practice, I am regaining some of those past skills. When facing challenging situations, I will rehearse in my mind or out loud what I want to say. To keep track of everything, I became queen of the Post-It notes, sticking them all around to remind myself of everything from a passing thought to a task to remember. Eventually I could have wallpapered a small room with all the notes I had lying around. Sometimes I put a note in a clever place so I wouldn't forget it, only to stumble upon it weeks later when the reminder no longer mattered. This wasn't working. My mental jumble spilled into my physical world.

John suggested using a notebook instead of all the Post-It notes. I know the Post-It notes were driving John, a neat freak, crazy—even though he never let on. He was right though; keeping a notebook helps me keep my ideas and projects sorted out.

Why Is It Still Happening—and Will It Ever Go Away?

We did a lot of research when it was apparent this "chemo brain" phenomenon was not subsiding. Some medical sources say chemo brain can last up to five years. Really? So, this means it will come to an end, and I'll have full, normal mental functioning? Um, no. We have yet to find any sort of declarative statement like that. Can they really know? Chemotherapy is different for everyone as it is tailor-made for the individual patient's specific cancer. My oncology team was very clear when they said the formula for my chemotherapy concoction was designed just for me. It stands to reason then that the side effects from my chemo treatments were also unique to me. Looking further at research, I discovered that I experience some symptoms of other people, but other symptoms I did not have at all. How would I know the difference between chemo brain and the onset of dementia or Alzheimer's? It appears the reality is only time will tell.

Exercise Your Mind!

There seem to be many experts who have the answers to help with memory—but beware of subscribing to every theory out there. Here are some of the things I did to retrain my mind and memory. Maybe you will find some of these useful. We may all be different, but chemo brain is our common problem. Each of these tips and tools has played a part in helping me cope with this animal.

Use technology! There are countless apps for your phone in the form of puzzles, games, and logic problems. Staring at that little screen is not for me, but I know many younger readers are super comfortable using their phones extensively, and if that works, go for it. My dad is a big puzzle book person. When we visit my parents, we find his puzzle books throughout the house. Puzzles, word searches, and crosswords stimulate the mind. Success at these will build confidence. Jigsaw puzzles are great, especially because there are countless levels of difficulty and designs. Like muscles in the body, the brain responds best to a variety of options rather than repetitive tasks. All forms of puzzles are great options; puzzle books are portable, and they can be put down and started up again easily.

Getting lost in a good book can take your mind and imagination on all sorts of adventures, and along the way, it can sharpen it. A suggestion that was successful for me was avoiding long, intense novels. I recommend starting with shorter books and stories centered in a genre you already like. During the fog and grog of treatment and early recovery, the difficulty was staying awake long enough to make any real progress in a book. Finding the focus to read even a sentence was tough—let alone retaining what I had just read. I'd often forget by the next day what I had already read and have to start over. Magazine articles, due to their brevity, are a great source of reading during and after chemo. No pressure to figure out where you left off!

Anything that stimulates your mind in new and different ways is beneficial. Taking art classes to expand my horizons served several purposes. All the variety of classes I tried, such as painting, color theory, and figure drawing have opened my mind to new opportunities and experiences. The classes got me out of the house, which had become my safe place, and I was becoming a bit paranoid about leaving. Finding the courage to go was as important as the stimulation the classes provided.

However, there was a price to pay. All too eager to get back to normal, I took on way too much. My brain shifted into overdrive while trying to process all these new concepts, and I quickly became overloaded. The biggest thing I got out of taking so many classes in a short period of time turned out to be the worst thing that could have happened: the creation of stress and anxiety that I did not need. Excitement quickly turned to dread because I was doing too much. Be careful about doing things in moderation so you can get the full enjoyment of whatever you are doing.

Let's Get Physical

Physical activity is one of the greatest ways to reduce stress and reset the mind. Exercise helps keep the mind clear, calm, and open. Some days, this mental outlet outweighed the physical benefits. Everyone has their favorite form of exercise—whether it is walking, running, doing yoga, taking fitness classes, or maybe weight training. Whatever it is, start with what you know. If treatments hit your body as hard as mine did, you may require physical therapy to retrain your muscles to work effectively again. No matter your physical state, start somewhere. Get moving! Just go for a walk. You have to learn to walk before you can run and soar.

Are there any solutions for chemo brain that come from a bottle? I've tried a multitude of supplements that are recommended to help sharpen the mind, but in my humble opinion, I haven't found anything that really worked for me. Others may swear by certain supplements to help cognition. The bottom line is to do your research, consult your physician, and you do you.

Organization Is the Key

My mind no longer works in an organized, linear format. And organization is, of course, crucial to almost everything. Things that have worked for me may seem simple, but this is about functioning. It is not rocket science. The beauty of the tips that follow is they are easy to implement and incorporate into your life.

Make a list! Lists are great for one major purpose: keeping focus on what needs to be accomplished daily, weekly, and monthly. Use a calendar, check it, and update it regularly. Lists are about keeping order and purpose. A great tool I use is keeping a journal. Journaling helps me chronicle and remember the important days, trips, and events in our lives. You may be surprised how often you go back to reference that journal.

Using word-association techniques to help remember things that are important is helpful. I try to create my own little acronyms. Most people will use "Roy G. Biv" to remember the colors of the rainbow: red, orange, yellow, green, blue, indigo, violet. I make up easy-to-remember words for lists I need to retain.

John and I are huge fans of the Zac Brown Band, and we are even part of their fan club. Some of their songs helped us escape the world we were living in for a bit. When I was bald, Zac even sent me some of the knit hats he was known for wearing on stage. When I leave the house, I often forget my phone, wallet, or keys. To help me remember, I use one of my favorite ZBB songs "As She's Walking Away." I change it to "As C's WALK-ing

Away," C for cell phone, WAL for wallet, and K for keys. Weird? Yes, but it works for me! Make an acronym that works for you!

Here is a big trick that I have really come to rely on. When John and I are out and run into someone who only I know, but I cannot recall their name, we have an agreement. If I don't introduce him to the person right away, John will introduce himself and ask the person's name. He has to do this quickly, so it doesn't look as if I have no idea who the person is. Then I just say, "Oh, gosh. I'm so sorry I didn't introduce you right away." This is a nice little trick, so I don't have to be embarrassed about not being able to recall their name.

No matter what, know that you may be contending with this for a long time to come. So, hang in there my fellow "chemo crew," you will get through this.

Lessons Learned

1. The key to dealing with chemo brain is to know it's real, it can happen, and you may be dealing with some challenges for a long time.
2. Keep calm and carry on. Use pauses and patience. Do not judge yourself for struggling through mental processes.
3. Do your research. Talk to your health care provider. They can't help you find solutions unless you are open and ask.
4. Read, exercise, meditate, and get your rest. Use your mind. Exercise it often. Your brain is like your other muscles; it needs to be fit. With practice, your mind will improve and become more fit—just like your body.
5. Organize your life to create your own support systems: lists, calendars, or using your phone for reminders and journaling. Organization is the key to success.
6. You may experience feelings of inadequacy and frustration when your mind does not work the way you want it to. Getting upset often causes symptoms to worsen. Pause, take a breath, and be kind to yourself!
7. You are a fighter! Keep fighting. Be proud of what you have overcome and where you are right now!

CHAPTER 7B: JOHN

Well, Tell Me, Who Are You?

Something Is Just Not Right

What happened to her brain? You know, not a day goes by where I don't ask that question to myself. Frankly, it's really difficult sometimes to see what Sherri is contending with as she fights a silent, invisible enemy in her brain. Ever since treatment ended, she has these gaps in her mental processing, and everything gets scrambled. These gaps do not last long, but they are enough to make her pause, lose her train of thought, and then struggle to find and sort out words. Moments later, the light comes on, and she finally can generate the word or words she wanted to say in the first place. Scatterbrained? No. It's just part of the processing she has to contend with.

Sherri is a brilliant woman and has so many gifts both professionally and personally. She has amazing intuition and insight, and she can react to a crisis instantly and know exactly what to do. She is a fantastic mom, has amazing compassion for others, and radiates an aura of positive energy. For as long as I have known her, people have been drawn to her. People want to know Sherri, and they love her positive energy, warm smile, and compassionate personality.

Cancer tried to snuff out that light. It failed. No way could it have succeeded in overcoming her willpower to live. Sherri beat cancer's ass, but there was a price to pay. Science was needed to combat that cancer. Science and medicine did what they were designed to do, but they also altered some things along the way. Her lungs are scarred and forever changed, and her mental functioning and processes have been impacted. Chemotherapy seemingly "scarred" her brain somehow. She lives with the effects of this every day. Will it ever subside? Will there ever come a day when there are no reminders of those harsh doses of chemo? Only time will tell.

Ask the questions!

Caregivers, ask the important questions! Particularly, be direct and specific in asking about long-term effects on the body and the brain. One of my big regrets was not asking those questions before, during, or after treatment. When we were in the moment, neither of us could have cared less about a year or two down the road. We only hoped Sherri would still be with us in the world. You do not think clearly about the future when the battle is at hand. Not that things would have been easier, but I thrive on preparedness, and knowing that Sherri was going to enter a world of short-term memory loss, confusion, and delayed response for years to come would certainly have been helpful.

Sherri's External Hard Drive

The oncologist said, "Since the cancer is growing fast, it can die fast." Those words were comforting. He was honest and divulged that the dosage would be progressively increased in each round of treatment. We know now that meant more potential issues later with the effects on the brain. Chemo impacted her short-term memory.

Many experiences that happened once she started chemo have been blurred, scrambled, or lost somewhere in her brain. It is not hard for me to see that she must keep trying to fill in those gaps, which frustrates her to no end, and it may continue to some degree for the rest of her life. One of the things I can help her with is filling in those gaps, refreshing her mind with memories, reminding her about information the doctors gave us, or even assisting her with organizing her calendar. Watching her struggle with this problem is a difficult reminder of how important my role as caregiver, in some ways, will never go away.

Before cancer, Sherri's mind was incredibly sharp, and it still catches me off guard when she cannot recall things. Losing patience is never the right option. Sometimes taking a few deep breaths and thinking before I speak goes a long way. Empathy is critical because she is more frustrated than I ever could be. There is no magic training plan; it simply requires awareness and self-discipline to allow her to work through her thoughts. Awareness means being in tune with how Sherri is feeling physically, mentally, and emotionally. Providing gentle reminders that fatigue exacerbates these pauses and gaps brings her awareness that she needs a break, but she often doesn't realize it when she's engrossed in an activity. Usually, she will just sigh and say, "OK." After she takes that break, I can visibly see the frustration lift.

Write It Down

Another important role is to help your loved one reestablish a sense of order and organization in their life. This will certainly vary from person to person, but at first, it could be a real demand on you as a caregiver.

Sherri has always kept a very organized calendar, and she keeps them from years past as a resource for recalling past events, appointments, etc. At first, I did not expect she would have trouble getting back into this habit. What I discovered was that she was indeed writing down upcoming appointments, but then she would not look at it again to see what was upcoming. It was almost an out of sight, out mind thing. She didn't even think to check it; there just was no memory trigger.

Once the calendar went back in her purse, she might not get it out again until it was time to write in a new date. This caused her to miss a few hair appointments, PT sessions, and even dinner with friends. She tried posting sticky notes around the house as reminders, but that didn't work because she had so many that it negated the desired outcome.

To help, I started planting seeds. On the weekends I would fill her in on my upcoming week and then ask what she had on her schedule for the coming week. This prompted her to look over her calendar and gave me a chance to ensure I also knew what she had. I had her keep a notebook of things to do that she kept out on the table to keep her reminders in one organized place. To help further, I put her appointments for everything in my phone. Finally, even though she is not a huge fan of tech, I encouraged Sherri to use her phone calendar and set reminder alerts.

Interestingly, chemo only seems to have impacted the short-term memory. It took me a while to realize this. Maybe because I was so busy being a caregiver that I never noticed. The stuff she *does* remember is astounding: people we haven't seen in years, places we have been long ago, distant childhood memories, and even trivia. The pattern was more noticeable as she became more independent, and I wasn't focused on helping her with daily activities and transporting her everywhere. What a crazy thing this chemo brain is. I gained real peace of mind when I got a better handle on the causes and symptoms and accepted that it is something we have to live with and work through. I knowing my role as her number one supporter.

Is There an End in Sight?

Will she ever come out of this entirely? The bottom line is we just do not know. Each individual's recovery will be as unique as their cancer and treatment plan. In the end, only time will answer our questions.

Takeaways: Chemo Brain Do's and Don'ts for Caregivers!

1. Listen to respond—not to react.
2. Do not continually correct memory lapses (unless asked).
3. Do not complete sentences when there is a pause as they search for the right word or phrase.
4. Do be patient and understanding. No matter what, allow your loved one to think and work it out themselves! Patience, my friends, above all else. Patience!
5. Do be empathetic and try to reverse roles.
6. Do not ever show you are growing impatient or annoyed. That will only exacerbate the anxiety and frustration they already feel.
7. Encourage them to stay active and busy and try new activities to stimulate the mind and muscle memory.
8. Always remember: As General George Patton said, and he was paraphrasing Shakespeare, "Fatigue makes cowards of us all." In other words, *know* that when your loved one is tired and exhausted, the condition will be more obvious, the delays will be longer, and the concern and anxiety will be heightened.
9. Let them vent whenever they need to.
10. Devise a plan together to help spur word and memory recall. Use environmental triggers in a positive way. For example, if she needs to remember to bring something to work the next day, she places it by the door or with her other things. Sticky notes are another reminder option. Obviously the best plan is whatever will work for your loved one, but know that both partners have a part to play.

CHAPTER 8A: SHERRI

I Want to Break Free!

Independence and Coming Out of My Bubble

I was 100 percent dependent on John. Having settled into this new role of the "girl in her bubble," my life was vastly different from the freedoms I used to know. My decline into dependency was gradual, but in recovery, the realization quickly set in that I had entirely lost my ability to function independently. I had been robbed of my freedom and my confidence. Gaining it back would prove to be emotional and scary, but each step was triumphant.

Outings were mostly limited to doctors' appointments and tests, and John always drove and attended them with me. Besides feeling exhausted, my immune system was extremely compromised by the chemo cocktail, which put me at risk out in public of getting exposed to all sorts of germs. Once discharged from the hospital for the last time, I was too weak to walk without the assistance of a walker. I began physical therapy, and I had to be driven to the appointments. Even after I ditched the walker, I was still too unsteady to drive.

Once I started chemotherapy, driving just became something I used to do. Drugs and chemo decimated my body, weakening me physically and mentally. Making the split-second decisions that are required when driving a car was beyond me at that time, and being behind the wheel was unsafe for me, the car, and anyone on the road.

I Can Drive!

Finally, the day came. I was going to drive myself to physical therapy. Freedom! Well, don't get too excited. We only lived three minutes from the PT clinic—five minutes if you get the traffic light. Still, it was just me, the car, and less than a mile of pavement! Starting the car felt like being a teenager again on my first solo ride. I was energized, thoroughly excited, and a little scared and apprehensive. *Do I still know how to do this? What if I forgot?*

Off I went, cruising down the street. Arriving at PT a whopping three minutes after getting in the car, I burst into the clinic, beaming with pride and bragging to everyone within earshot that I had driven myself to physical therapy!

When it was time to drive home, thoughts of going back into my bubble filled me with dread. Then, what should come on the radio? Only a familiar metal song from the eighties that we all jammed to. "All aboard … ha-ha-ha-ha!" It was Ozzy Osbourne's "Crazy Train." With the windows and sunroof wide open and the radio cranked up, I drove carefree a whole mile through the neighborhood. Yahoo! I did not care that it was drizzling and forty degrees out. To me, it was a ninety-degree July day, and I felt free and alive. That was just the catalyst needed to help me realize how much I craved independence.

Shopping, Cooking, and Cleaning

When our boys lived at home, they seemed to have bottomless pits for stomachs. They always wanted to eat, and going to the grocery store was a frequent occurrence and a place I knew quite well. Being such a familiar place, I thought the grocery store would be a great option to test the waters in trying to integrate back into life.

The first time going to the store together was an epic failure. I didn't expect all the stimuli to be bombarding my senses all at once. It was overwhelming. Without realizing it, I stuck close to John. I was like a duckling following the mother duck.

He quickly noticed my apprehension about being in a big box store and cleverly gave me little manageable "tasks" to complete. My first "excursion" was a trip to the deli counter to get lunch meat. Comprehending the simple questions posed at the deli counter "How much did you say you wanted?" or "How would you like that sliced?" made me want to turn around and run away.

Internally, I recognized the struggle, paused to center myself, and took a deep breath to calm my mind, which allowed me to process the questions and complete the order. As I helped fill our cart with other items, the products would get jumbled up in my brain. I couldn't differentiate between a bag of frozen corn and frozen beans. It was like the bags were jumping out at me. The experience was completely overwhelming. Still, just putting myself out in the world again was a big step. With each excursion, the overwhelmed feeling lessened—and my confidence improved.

John took over all the cooking and meal prepping for the longest time. Though I was ready to chip in, there were apprehensions. The thought of following a recipe, correctly measuring ingredients, or even the safety concerns of cutting myself with a knife or leaving the stove on were enough to give me pause. Start simple! To combat those apprehensions, I prepared simple meals that didn't require recipes or measurements. Gradually I was able prepare a multicourse meal again, but even to this day, I sometimes get stuck on a measurement or two.

When looking to rebuild physical and mental strength, even starting to pitch in with chores or cleaning the house provided a sense of empowerment and taking my life back. Treatment leaves us helpless, often confined in our own homes, for a long time. Cleaning the house does so much more than removing dust from the floor; it also removes stains of helplessness that settle in our minds. Contributing again and making a difference, for the first time in a year, I was able to help take care of my home. It was exhausting—but wonderful—and life was good!

Going It Alone

The next logical step was going to the grocery store by myself. Before going, it was important to set myself up for success. I sat at the kitchen table and made an entire list, but the list was according to how everything was arranged at the store. If I were going to do this, it would be important to walk into the store with a plan that would work for me. It was a *great* day! That day was not about the shopping; the day signified the start back to independence and taking joy in the small victories.

Fries or Freak-Out?

Part of winning back my independence had a by-product: panic attacks. In one instance at a restaurant, while everyone was talking and laughing, the waitress started asking for everyone's order. The panic was rising because, just like reading a recipe, I couldn't sort out the words to even read the menu. My mind could not grasp what the pictures were. I was frozen.

John saw me struggling, and he quietly pointed out the types of foods I liked, which helped me make a choice. He helped me discreetly make a choice and, once we ordered, I was fine. No one else realized the panic I felt. In the end, I was able to make my meal choice on my own. Chalk up another small victory.

It would have been easy to stay home and in the protective cocoon created by the illness. Forcing myself to take risks was difficult, but I found getting out again—while both terrifying and liberating—was absolutely necessary. It was therapy, and every new adventure was a hurdle to overcome on the road toward recovery. If I can give any direction to you, it is this: the road back to a confident, clear-thinking mind is long and hard. Baby steps are required, and thinking you can just resume your old normal will only leave you disappointed. Celebrate the small victories. Use every opportunity to step outside your comfort zone just a little bit further than the last time.

Laughter Is the Best Medicine

All the little things, like the daily life activities that we take for granted, were just so important to do again. The dark cloud of cancer was finally lifting as I began to do more and reclaim my independence. One thing I missed was genuine laughter. Studies show that laughter really is good medicine; it helps prevent disease and hastens recovery.

We didn't have a lot to smile about for a long time because one complication after another was hurled at me. I needed to laugh again. I wanted to laugh hysterically to the point of tears. Laughter would be a sign to me that I was breaking the chains of cancer and that the dark clouds were lifting.

The first time I really belly laughed again was at dinner with a couple of close friends John and I had known since our kids were young. We ate dinner and laughed. We talked and told stories, and we laughed. My belly hurt from laughing so hard—and thankfully not once did anyone ask how I was doing.

Back to Work!

Going to work every day like the rest of the world would serve as proof that I was on the mend. After nearly a year, I was back on the job. Prior to starting back, I met with my supervisor to discuss how to phase back into the routine. Naturally, I decided to jump in with both feet and start back full-time, working the entirety of the days.

True independence was here! Going back to work meant being back as a full participant in life. The day I returned to work was naturally filled with nerves and excitement. Upon leaving the house, I stopped just before opening the door to leave and looked around at the house. This house had been my refuge, my bubble, and at times, my prison. Tears of joy and relief streamed down my face. Walking out the door marked the end of my cancer treatments. Working again was a major milestone. My recovery was in full swing, and cancer was becoming something that happened—not something that defined me.

When I arrived at work that first day, I was showered with balloons, cards, hugs, and even roses John had sent to my school. I was thrilled to be back. My hair was just beginning to sprout, and one secretary even got a buzz cut to stand in solidarity with me! Kindness and warmth were shown to me by everyone. The day was exhausting, but I left with a full heart, feeling the love of a community that was behind me. I was back!

You Can Let Go Now

Wanting my independence back created an unexpected power struggle between John and me. All throughout the illness and treatment, he was the caregiver—and I relinquished my independence and almost all the decision-making to him. We had always been equal partners, but to beat cancer, I needed to exist in my bubble to fight, heal, and survive.

When my strength and confidence finally began returning—and I was ready to spread my wings and take flight from the nest—John still wanted to do everything for me. Though his help was coming from a place of love, I was ready to find myself again and be the new, independent me. Gradually, it began to get under my skin when he wouldn't let go, and it became irritating when he continued to make decisions for me and didn't let go.

So, what did I do? I purposely chose the opposite thing he was going to choose for me. Throughout illness and early in recovering, John did it all for me—simple things like deciding our menu, picking clothes to wear, and deciding what I should drink and eat for a snack—when I could not. Even though he was glad I was better, I believe he was so used to me needing to lean on him so much that it was hard for him to let go. In some ways, I felt guilty for wanting my independence back. He had taken such unselfish loving care of me, and I didn't want to hurt his feelings or make him think I didn't love or need him anymore.

Instead of talking about it, I decided to be difficult, figuring he would get the hint. If he said carrots, I said peas. If he said black, I said white. Even if I didn't mean it, I would purposely say the opposite just to be my own person. I was tired of being hovered over. Even if I was out of the room seemingly too long, he would call for me to see if I was OK. Sometimes I purposely would not answer to see how long it would take for him to come and find me.

One day, I finally just had to tell him, quite firmly, to let me do things myself. He got the message and slowly began to give me leeway, though he did need a few more reminders. Had I not spoken up, it may have caused our relationship to morph into one where we weren't equal partners anymore, which could have led to some potentially deep resentment down the road. Being up front and direct with each other has always been a foundation of our marriage, and I know it is one reason our marriage has always been a strong one.

So, Why Am I Not Feeling Joy?

All this new independence was great, and settling back into the daily grind of the job wasn't as hard as I thought it would be. Work was going well. It was challenging my mind and keeping me busy and engaged.

As I was driving home, a cloud of melancholy enveloped me. This was simply not normal. What was wrong with me? I should be grateful for everything around me, but instead, I felt sad and empty. This went on for several months where my great mood at work didn't match the sadness I was feeling at home. For no apparent reason, my mood was somber—and John got the brunt of it. How could I be sad to come home to our house and John? Yet, there I was in this unexplainable funk.

Confused by these feelings, I did some soul-searching about what exactly was so dreadful about being at home. Then it hit me; it was the house! The energy of the house was depressing. To me, our house had become a place where I had been sick, ailing, and confined. The walls were taupe, and our furniture was brown, and along with being stuck in these surroundings, the house felt like a dungeon. We decided to change the energy of our house and transform it into an inviting space that was full of positive vibes.

It was time to transform the environment and redecorate! It was long overdue anyway. Feng shui is a concept for decorating that uses energy forces to bring balance and harmony to a person and their living environment. Since we wanted a bright and happy home, we lightened all the walls and bought all new light-colored furniture.

The new decor was full of vibrant, uplifting colors. These simple changes really helped bring a renewed sense of home to the house. Brighter, colorful, and more cheerful, the house had a new energy. It felt like home and not just a house.

The final touch was a sage cleansing. Negative energy can accumulate in a home and drag down its energy. Taking a bundle of white sage and burning it allows the smoke to circulate in every room and every corner, helping eliminate the negative energy. This simple ceremony gave me an empowered sense of interaction with my environment. Whether it truly worked or symbolically worked cannot be proven, but our house now has a sense of joy and serenity filling its walls. It is truly home.

Lessons Learned

1. Baby steps count! You are still moving forward. It may be scary taking those first steps, but you cannot learn to run until you can walk.
2. Your independence will come—but bring it back gradually. Have a plan for easing back into life. Allow yourself to experience the process, and along the way, you will build confidence in your ability to accomplish even the smallest tasks. You may have the entire marathon in front of you, but it all starts with the first step.

3. Appreciate the mundane things in life. Nothing is mundane when you are unable to do it. I found out the hard way to appreciate cooking, cleaning, and shopping. Take nothing for granted.

4. Be assertive and up front about your goal of being independent. Never be afraid to have conversations with your loved ones. When you are ready, be honest and direct: "No, I'll do it myself." Do not compromise your freedom or simply exist at the whim of others.

5. Be kind and accepting of yourself. Independence may not come as quickly as you would like—so celebrate every victory!

6. Easing back into work can be scary. To lessen your anxiety, set up a meeting with your supervisor. Be up front about where you are physically, mentally, and emotionally—and get a grasp on their expectations for you.

7. Change the environment. Surround yourself with positive affirmations at home, at work, and everywhere you go—right down to the design and decor. Your home is where your heart lies; make it a special place of happiness and serenity.

CHAPTER 8B: JOHN

Not the Rock I Once Was

Letting Go of Control: She's Back!

Juggling work and household duties around Sherri's appointments, procedures, and crises, I found myself also making all the major decisions. For example, if we had been remodeling and painting during her treatments, she would have zero interest in deciding colors and designs. If we had needed to revisit our investments or meet with our financial advisor, I would have been alone. Sherri got to the point where it didn't matter, and she didn't care about any of these decisions. I would simply give her nuggets of info about what was going on, but she was much more focused on navigating this abyss of recovery, which was all she needed or wanted on her plate.

So, in the midst of all the treatments, side effects, and complications, pretty much everything in our lives was up to me. The problem is that once I grab hold of the wheel, I have a hard time letting go. My years as a leader of others meant making key decisions, and it included being a protector. And in this place and time, I most definitely was in a position of control and protecting Sherri. As her caregiver, I had to be her rock and her protection.

"I Can Do This Myself!"

After Sherri finally was able to come home, she was just a shadow of herself. She was missing the substance. In her weakened state, she was unable to do a whole lot for herself beyond the basics of human necessity. I made every effort to ensure her comfort and make sure she was doing everything she was supposed to do in her recovery.

One day, she wanted to test the waters and start doing some of the mundane household chores herself while I was at school. And then, the big one was she wanted to drive. *Shit! She isn't ready for that is she? No way.* That is where I made another mistake.

Letting go was not going to be easy. Clearly, I was not ready to cut the cord. As she regained her strength and began to spread her wings, I was oblivious to her growing desire for independence. I had settled into this role of doing everything. My apprehension set in when I discovered she did something herself, questioning not only if she was OK, but did she do it right? Am I going to have to go back and redo it? That was the control freak in me. Her feelings had to be hurt, but I never noticed.

As she was now ready to fly, I could not see that I was holding her back. When she drove herself to a PT appointment, even though I was glad she was going to do it, I was a nervous wreck. I had asked her to text me when she was leaving home and when she arrived at PT. Naturally, she remembered to do neither—thanks to that damn chemo brain!

When she called me after she got home, with all the excitement of a kid whose team had just won the championship, I must confess that, though elated for her, I felt a little empty inside. She was starting to fly solo, and she wouldn't need me to do everything much longer. Before long, she would be driving everywhere on her own, shopping, and attending exercise classes. It really was amazing to see the rejuvenation of her independent spirit, but there would be some confusion along the way.

I Don't Know My Role Anymore

In my defense, letting go was made more difficult by mixed messages from Sherri. When I finally realized that she wanted independence, I started to back off. On one hand, though she was getting herself signed up for new activities and events, as the day approached to attend them, she expected me to go along or to act as chauffeur. She wanted me, in some cases, to do the activity with her and be there for moral support. Ultimately, I always went out of concern for her safety and well-being—and maybe because I still wanted her to need me. My new role was quite unclear. At home, she wanted to take on more duties and wanted me to back off my mother hen-like behavior. Did she need me to be a helicopter husband—or would she rather fly solo?

Setting Me Straight

Our relationship had become reminiscent of a yo-yo. One minute, she was tight in hand, wanting support, and the next, she was fully extended, free to spin. Up and down we went, playing this game of independence versus dependency. Finally, we both had had enough. I don't recall the issue or the time, but Sherri put her foot down and shouted at me to stop telling her how to do everything. "No more hovering!" It was a transformative moment for Sherri. Honestly, it was liberating for both of us!

To revisit that time—and I have no desire to—and do it all again, our communication should have been better. We should have sat down and discussed what she thought she was ready to do on her own versus when she wanted help. I should have helped her set small, manageable goals for tasks and activities. A sense of purpose and targeted goals for independence would have really been a great idea and given us both the direction we needed to successfully work through that time. We needed to verbalize our expectations for ourselves and each other.

Takeaways

1. Communicate! Unless you are mind readers, you need to have regular candid conversations throughout the recovery process.
2. Be prepared for them to soar one day and want to fly solo—but then want to be tucked away safely in the nest the next day, with you watching over them.
3. Body language: read it! Watch for signs. Learn when to provide subtle support and when to get out of the way, especially in public and social situations.
4. Finally, in those moments when they are feeling independent, give them a nudge instead of holding them back. Then step back and enjoy it! This is what you both want.

CHAPTER 9A: SHERRI

I Get Knocked Down, But I Get Up Again

Get Up and Move!

As if having cancer isn't enough, the post-chemo side effects are vicious and do not want to release their hold, leaving an indelible mark like a tattoo. The degree of residual damage may vary in its severity, becoming a temporary or even permanent part of life. For myself, there are the visible surgical scars to my body, but the real scarring and damage was done to my lungs from the lymphoma and treatments. Every cough is a constant reminder of the ordeal.

To remain healthy, it is imperative that I challenge my lungs by working out. Keeping them strong will help me fight off future pathogens and irritants my lungs may be exposed to. Exercise is a key component to maintaining a healthy, active life. It is a nonnegotiable part of my daily routine. My body was ravaged by treatments, and I was dependent on a walker—so accepting this as my reality was important mentally. I needed to be kind to myself and acknowledge that baby steps need to be celebrated. Pushing too hard would only set me up for failure both physically and mentally. No matter my starting point, the important thing was that I started! The bottom line is to continue exercising and not give up.

Dancin' to the Oldies

During recovery, I decided to join the "Silver Sneakers" brigade. Silver Sneakers is a fitness program designed for people who are sixty-five and older. I love dancing and music, and attending a dance class for my first exercise class was an easy choice.

With a ball cap to cover my still bald head, it was off to the YMCA. I found a space in the back of the gym, hoping no one would notice me.

Everyone was a regular, and they spotted the newbie right away. Once my hat came off, it didn't matter that I was bald. People came up to me from every part of the room to welcome me. There was no judgment or pity—only complete acceptance. As the music started, with arms waving and bodies moving, we danced our hearts out. I was in the right place.

These simple movements quickly exposed the obvious. My brain and body were not connecting, and it did not take long to realize the classes might be too much for me. My mind saw and heard the instructor, but the message did not get to my muscles until we had already moved on to the next step. I wobbled and flailed, but I kept on going; it was so very frustrating to not be able to do simple moves that used to be effortless.

After a few moments of getting mad and upset at my crazy, out-of-sync moves, I stopped, took a deep breath, and decided to celebrate the fact that I had even made it to the place where I could dance again. I almost allowed myself to slip into self-criticism and leave disappointed, but these people were having a great time. When I looked around, many others were just as out of sync as I was! In that moment, I learned not to judge myself and recognize that all I really needed to do was simply enjoy the class and allow my body and mind to get to know each other again. This class wasn't about the dance routine; it was so much bigger than that. After several weeks of classes, the day finally came when I was stronger. It was time to move on and get back to more rigorous classes. Away I went!

Yoga!

Yoga was a big part of my pre-cancer fitness regimen. The mindfulness skills and meditative practices have always been a boost to my soul. While battling the lymphoma, these mindfulness skills came in handy. Controlled breathing and meditation helped me endure some tough procedures and difficult days. I was excited to get back onto a mat and do my first downward facing dog in ages.

In my very first post-treatment yoga class, we flowed into a simple lunge pose, and next thing I knew, my ankle gave out. I was on the floor—lying on someone else's mat! It was one of those awkward moments where time stands still. The instructor stopped the class and made it a huge event to find out if I was OK. I wanted to crawl under a yoga mat and disappear!

It would have been so easy to run out of that room, crying and embarrassed, but why? What would that prove? Instead, I smiled, said, "Namaste" (a yogi greeting for peace), and went proudly back to my mat. That was a key moment for me. I could either leave the class feeling ashamed and demoralized (I was tempted for sure), or smile, laugh, and love the fact that I could even be there in the first place. If I hadn't stayed to overcome that fall, it could have been amplified in my mind. That incident could have spiraled into something much worse than it was. I might have never gone back.

Breathing Isn't as Easy as It Looks

So much of yoga is focused on the breath. When stuck in stressful moments and scenarios that we can't control, if we just focus and control our breathing, we can face a situation with poise and calm. But there was a time when that advice did not work for me.

Just before getting diagnosed and plagued with that awful cough, I would find myself in yoga class, chest tight and constricted, coughing and hacking. Sipping water and keeping a steady supply of cough drops in my mouth was often the only way to make it through a class. I got to the point of dreading the Savasana part of yoga: the last pose of peace and relaxation while lying on your back. It's usually the best part of class! For me, lying flat always caused ferocious coughing fits, and I would sometimes need to step out of the room to avoid disturbing the other yogis.

You can't take the breath out of yoga. In returning to yoga, when the instructor would start the class by drawing awareness to our breath, panic would set in. It took me right back to my coughing fits at the time of diagnosis. I had to adapt. If I couldn't conquer my fear of the breath in the yoga studio, it would be easier for fear to take over in other areas of my life. To get past my issues with the breathing, I began focusing on having a strong heartbeat, the emotional aspect of the heart, all the people I love, the things I love about them, and other positive mantras. In life, we cannot always remove challenges, but we can come up with adaptations.

Eventually, with time and persistence, breath work didn't bother me anymore. Today, I'm totally engaged in my breath—and I am so grateful for the use of my lungs.

Running Again!

Do your exercises! It took a lot of PT, long walks, and a lot of skinned knees, but I eventually started running again. In truth, it was actually more of a floppy walk. I started slowly, but soon three minutes turned into five, and eventually five minutes became a mile! People driving by were giving me looks, probably wondering if they needed to stop because I looked like I was about to collapse. The memory of getting sick while training for a half-marathon lived firmly in my mind, but I thought, *You know what? I need to run another race.*

I Am a Savage!

For weeks, I thought, *Who are you kidding? You can't do this race!*

On the morning of a Savage obstacle race we had entered—even up to the moment of the starting gun—I wasn't going to do it.

As John was standing there waiting for the gun to go off, I was overwhelmed with a surge of determination. My inner voice resoundingly said, "You can do this, you will do this, you *need* to do this!"

I jumped in next to him, and off we went on the first challenge: racing to the top of a ski mountain. In central Ohio, a "ski mountain" is actually more of a little hill, but in that moment, I was running up Mount Everest! Did I successfully complete every obstacle? Heck no! But did I try? Yes! And did I finish? You better believe I did! John and I ran across the finish line hand in hand, and we both had tears of joy running down our faces because it was a huge victory in taking my life back.

Some people say, "Be grateful for what you can do—be grateful that you are here." I get that, but I wanted more. Living out my years just walking through life, afraid and worrying about what could happen, wasn't really living. It was just existing. Those tears as we crossed the finish line were not just about all those times I could barely walk, I fell, or I had trouble breathing; that finish line was actually more of a starting point for the rest of my life.

Had I just accepted that I was a frail shadow of my old self, those tears would have been ongoing through my life. Digging deep is what won the day. In the end, we only have ourselves to rely on. I had a choice to make that day, and our choices have consequences. One choice can set us up for everything we will face from that moment forward. I didn't give up when I had cancer. I wasn't going to let it beat me or stop me from fully living. I am alive and well!

Lessons Learned

1. Tom Petty and the Heartbreakers' "I Won't Back Down" became my mantra. The song is all about resilience. All those times when I could have succumbed to fear, I remembered these lines:

    > Well, I won't back down.
    > No, I won't back down.
    > You can stand me up at the gates of hell,
    > But I won't back down.

    If you let fear stop you from taking a first step, it will be harder and harder to take the steps needed to move forward. Excuses will rule the day, and they will become your reality. You are powerful. You are strong. Embrace your inner power.

2. "Just do it," as Nike says. For you, the "it" may just be getting up out of a chair by yourself or dancing like no one's around. Listen to your body through intuitive movement. Just move with no set plan. Your body knows what it needs; you just need to listen. Movement lowers stress and builds confidence. Even if you fall, get back up and forge ahead. Nelson Mandela said, "Do not judge me by my success—judge me by how many times I fell down and got back up again."

3. Have patience for your "new" body and know there may be some limitations. If you don't get to know your body, you can't accept this amazing new you.

4. Do something you enjoy, start slow, and show yourself kindness. Take a class, discover a new hobby, update your wardrobe, or buy new shoes. Do something fun that makes you feel good. Treat yourself—you deserve it.

5. Change your perspective. Instead of saying, "Look what happened to me," flip it to "I get to discover a better me that is full of new possibilities!" It is a gift to overcome a life-threatening illness and get a second chance at life. It changes everything.

6. Resilience means many things to many people. For me, it meant getting over what I had lost—the old me—and accepting a new reality. Resist if you want, but you'll do nothing but mourn what you've lost. If you pick yourself up, accept that you have a new reality, and reconcile with what you have lost, you will ultimately find a new purpose in your life.

CHAPTER 9B: JOHN

I Just Love Baby Giraffes!

Getting Her Body Back—Her Way

Sherri always loved the fact that she could beat me in a long-distance race. She didn't rub it in much, but she always had this look of pride when she finished first on a run. For as long as we have been together as a couple, we have been into fitness. While strength training is my thing, Sherri really kicks butt in just about everything else. It doesn't help that I'm built like Clydesdale and Sherri is more of a gazelle, giving her a slight advantage. But, hey, no excuses, right?

Coming Home Post-Treatment

When Sherri left the hospital after her last treatment, she was using a walker. There are ninety-year-olds and centenarians who are more stable than Sherri, only fifty years old, was at that time. Hard to believe it had been just a few years earlier that we watched her complete the last sixteen miles of a marathon on a broken leg! I had an incredible surge of emotion and disbelief the day they wheeled her out to the car from the hospital lobby. I knew in that instant how huge my role would be in helping her regain her strength and functioning.

Helping Sherri back to a level of active independence was a must. Her healing and recovery would only improve with increases in her strength and stamina. She had weeks of physical therapy ahead. At that time, my approach was entirely one of "let's take our time," but she was highly motivated to ditch that walker and get back to moving on her own without assistance. I already mentioned how stubborn and driven she is.

A Baby Giraffe Lives Here

Sherri did indeed ditch that walker in short order. However, her body and muscles were still weak; she simply was not stable. It did not take long for her to get to the point where a walker or cane were no longer necessary, but at the same time, I certainly would not let her walk along a narrow path on the edge of a cliff. There were times on walks where I would walk behind her, and the way she was moving made me feel as if we were in a small boat on rough seas. Sometimes she would start to go off balance and almost freeze halfway into a fall, and then she would slowly correct herself and avoid the topple. Our son Brian would always say, "Way to go, Mom. You stuck the landing!"

When we would go for walks, Sherri would often have to hold on to my arm for stability as she marched along. The oddest thing that was that whenever she turned her head, her legs would start to walk that way. I would have to pull her back onto the sidewalk; otherwise, she would start drifting into the grass. If something caught her eye on the other side of the street, she might drift off into it. At some point, I started referring to Sherri as my newborn giraffe. Baby giraffes wobble all over the place until they develop their strength and coordination. Now I had my own wobbly newborn giraffe in the house to take care of.

Not So Fast, Mister

Being supportive and encouraging is a vital component of caregiving. Caregiving doesn't end when the treatments stop, but knowing when to ease up and give some space was not my strong suit. That coach and control freak in me kept surfacing. My advice to any caregiver is to do a daily assessment of where things are and then know what is needed from you and what is not. Sometimes, instead of lending a hand or just letting her determine what she could handle, I pushed her too hard, eager to see her return to her old self. My philosophy was that the sooner she got back to her fitness regimen, the better. I look back now and realize that the obvious course was taking it slow and steady, one day at a time.

When she headed back to work full-time, I lost a little bit of "connectedness" to Sherri, and my awareness of her progress was diminished. Ultimately, I thought she was progressing faster than she really was, and I began to pressure her to take fitness classes, strength train at the YMCA, or get on a treadmill. In my mind, the marathon runner was still there; she just needed a coach to encourage her.

I went out and bought a treadmill for her that Christmas, and I was always trying to get her to use it. Misreading her state of mind, I was expecting her to do too much, too fast, stupidly forgetting the trauma she had been through and the state of her body and lungs.

Finally, she set me straight. She told me to stop pressuring her into an uncomfortable situation. I was blinded by the goal of getting her back to full strength and getting our lives back. What I was missing was what would happen if it did not go well; her self-confidence and belief in herself would plummet. Lesson revisited: these things take time.

The Mental-Physical Connection

From a mental perspective, Sherri was still reeling from all she had been through. So, why did it not occur to me that the mental and the physical were linked? She was living with huge amounts of fear and self-doubt, and she was in a constant state of anxiety that the cancer would come back with a vengeance. Her body was still reeling from the effects of chemo, and she fatigued quickly.

Fear, nerves, and anxiety are highly elevated when you are tired, exhausted, and in need of quality rest. Of course, she wanted to be well, be strong, and join me in an active lifestyle again. It became important to understand that she had to regain her confidence and build her mental strength along with her physical strength. How could I not see this right away? My entire approach and strategy to help her recover and get her life back had to take on a whole new look. The change in my approach was as important for Sherri mentally as it was physically.

What Do You Want to Do Today?

That is how any conversation with Sherri started from that point on. It was crystal clear that she, not I, had to be in control of her physical recovery. If Sherri initiated the conversation by saying that she wanted to do something regarding fitness or movement, I wisely responded, "OK, what did you have in mind?" Occasionally she would ask me for suggestions, but I took a more reserved role in the process and found that her "owning" this made all the difference in the world.

Walkin' the Beach

One of our favorite things to do on any beach vacation is to walk on the beach. I booked a brief getaway to warmer weather, hoping it would be therapeutic for Sherri. I believed it could work wonders in terms of helping her get stronger as we would trudge in and out of shallow water and walk on soft sand and the slope of the beach. Long walks on the beach in the surf could help improve core strength, balance, and muscle tone.

As soon as we arrived, we hit the sand almost immediately. The first time we went on a beach walk, the "baby giraffe" needed some guidance and a helping hand, but by the end of our week, even Sherri noticed how much better she was doing in terms of core and leg strength and stability.

Big win there! No matter what options you have, just get your loved one out of the house if you can! Go to the park, even if a drive is required, to get somewhere with some mildly tougher terrain. Bottom line? Do something that requires movement and activity. The impact of physical improvement reaped rewards, and her mental confidence started to soar.

Don't Worry about How Much: Just Enjoy and Celebrate It!

Relinquishing control and giving her space empowered her in so many ways. It wasn't *what* she was doing, how long she was doing it, or how intense; all that mattered was that she decided what she would do each day and be grateful that she could. It became my role to support and celebrate. When she came home all excited about Silver Sneakers fitness classes with the senior citizens, we celebrated, which only encouraged her to keep going since she enjoyed it.

When she outgrew the Silver Sneakers and "graduated" out of physical therapy, she wanted more. And it was something to behold; anyone could see that Sherri was getting stronger. Physically and mentally! She was visibly more confident, smiling again, and she was getting that glow back. Sherri always had an amazing energy radiating from her. People have noticed it for as long as I have known her. It all but disappeared during that ordeal, but it was coming back.

Just Encourage

In a matter of weeks, Sherri was ready to lace up her sneakers and get back into the race. She began signing up for fitness classes and started to go back to yoga. To inspire and encourage her, I tried other strategies such as small surprises like new workout gear here and there to pump her up. Sometimes the smallest gestures can be really uplifting. I was ecstatic when Sherri wanted to do a challenging "Savage" race. For as long as I live, I'll never forget that moment when she came running out to the starting line at the last second. It was priceless.

Knowing My Role

In hindsight, it is clear that Sherri's gradual return to activity was really about patience for both of us—and restraint on my part. I was not a football coach, and she was not one of my players. She was a recovering cancer survivor, and I was her husband and caregiver. The lesson here is to know the right roles to play and then let logic rule the day. In the end, what Sherri wanted and what she needed had to be the driving forces—not me trying to make decisions for her. My role was to be a supportive husband and caregiver, which was all she needed.

Takeaways

1. Do what you must, when you must, but also know when to get out of the way. There is a time to coach, a time to cheer, and a time to step back. Then, like any good coach, put them in the game—and let them show what they can do!
2. Let them determine what they need and want. The caregiver cannot own this; the survivor must.
3. Just be supportive.

CHAPTER 10A: SHERRI

I Can't Believe My Family and Friends Are Going to Read This!

Romance, Intimacy, and Sex

It's not like I forgot how. I just had zero desire to try. Zilch. We're talking about intimacy here, people—sex. Oh, it isn't that I didn't want to in my heart. I craved that feeling of romance and intimacy that two people deeply in love feel for each other, but the fire was squelched, extinguished, kaput!

Before cancer, our intimacy thrived. Of course, there were those times when it was less frequent due to life and schedules and demands of work, but we always seemed to find our way back to the passion we have for each other. We have always enjoyed doing most things together and have much more in common than not. This made becoming empty nesters an easy and enjoyable transition in our lives. It hasn't been perfect—nor are we—but we are best friends and soul mates. When the house was suddenly empty, it wasn't difficult for us to revert to the "pre-kids" years of our marriage. We certainly didn't run naked through the house like two cupids shooting arrows, but the flames were certainly burning bright again. Life was wonderful!

Not in the Mood

Throughout the months preceding a correct diagnosis, I did not realize how much our love life went right down the tubes. Intimacy dropped significantly. It was never the old "not tonight, I have a headache." It was more like "ZZZZZ." I was already asleep when John came to bed. I did not really feel "sick" all the time, but I just had no energy. I was constantly worrying about my persistent cough and what I might have going on in my lungs.

The effects of worry and anxiety are well-documented, especially when additional factors beyond everyday stressors are thrown into the mix. Hello, cancer and chemo. Let's put out a big welcome to the anxiety and worry and say goodbye to arousal and desire! This meant one thing for me: sex was not going to happen.

We Can Do It during Treatment? You Must Be Kidding!

During treatment, they tell you that if you are going to have sex, make sure your partner wears a condom or barrier device. If not, they literally would be exposing their "parts" to the chemo. We were informed at the hospital that chemotherapy can be excreted in vaginal secretions for forty-eight to seventy-two hours after a treatment. It's safe to say that "nuclear dick" was not something John wanted to experience. Sadly, condom wearing never even became an issue for us. When I wasn't in treatment, I was at home, feeling ill, nauseated, and fatigued while mentally preparing myself for the next round. The desire was gone. Sex couldn't have been further from my mind.

Why would John even want me? I lost my hair and had surgical scars and even a colostomy bag attached to my stomach, which routinely filled up with uh, well, shit. When looking in the mirror, I would just stare in disbelief at what my physical appearance had become. *Who is that person—and how did this become me?*

Sexual self-esteem is a real concept. Feeling attractive and desirable is an important part of the equation when it comes to arousal and sex. When we become so preoccupied with treatment, or more importantly, fighting for our lives, how can we even feel sexual self-esteem? When the medical team says you are finished with treatment, you get the "survivor speech." They did not say one thing about getting back to "normal" living or how I would feel physically and emotionally as I recovered. There was no mention of intimacy; it clearly was not on their checklist. Afterall, their priority was saving my life.

A Lack of Sensation

As my strength returned, it was quite apparent that things didn't work the way used to. One might say "the flower wasn't wilted; it was quite dreadfully dead." The clitoris has thousands of nerve endings. Wow! The lack of sensation was shocking considering how sensitive and powerful that small area is. A webinar we watched on sexual health through the hospital was eye-opening, and it was somewhat comforting to learn the effects of cancer treatment were a major factor in the issues I was having. It wasn't something I was doing wrong. Cancer and treatment can cause vaginal atrophy and dryness, resulting in decreased lubrication and a thinner vaginal wall.

When John became frisky, I went into a silent "Oh no!" panic mode. I had no urge and felt as though Novocain had been injected into my female parts; the area was completely numb. I found myself becoming distant and avoiding any sort of touch. I did not want him to think if I did give a hug or a kiss that I wanted it to lead to sex.

Seeking Help

I was so frustrated, and I know that John, though he was patient and never let on, had to be as well. I decided to broach the subject with my oncology team. Their reaction caught me off guard: "No one has ever asked," they said.

Maybe they hadn't been asked because they deal in lymphoma and not reproductive cancers. I was stunned. The survivorship program through the hospital was suggested as a place to turn. Survivorship offered an interesting lecture about physical changes after chemo, but no real solutions to intimacy and sexual dysfunction were addressed. Trust me, I already knew most of the effects; I was living them every day! Was there no one in modern medicine who could help? I needed solutions—not merely explanations.

Maybe the Tropics Will Start My Fire

Hoping to leave the cancer show in Ohio, we took a special trip to the Caribbean to enjoy the sun, sand, and sea. Maybe the sexual energy, once we were there, would build. Having some success right away might get the monkey off our backs, but it only made things more stressful and awkward when our first attempt failed.

What was the hurry? I don't know, actually. We certainly felt a sense of urgency and wanted to make it happen. Perhaps it was a fear that if we didn't try, we would just give up, losing that part of our marriage forever. I am sure the thought crossed our minds, but we were trying too hard and putting a lot of pressure on ourselves.

The opportunity to try again presented itself. We just sort of let it happen, not trying to force anything, and we finally made love. It was wonderful. The waves of the sea weren't the only waves crashing in that moment. No, the biggest wave of all was a tidal wave of relief. Neither of us can recall if we were intimate again on that trip, and I can tell you, things didn't just go back to the way it was before cancer, but in that moment, it didn't matter. We were overjoyed that the intimacy of our marriage was rekindled—and there was hope that maybe, just maybe, we could get back to the "old us." Cancer tried to take that from us, but we were able to answer, "Not so fast."

Night Sweats? Oh No!

All oncology checkups begin with questions, including, "Are you having night sweats?" Oddly, I never had night sweats, which are a classic sign of lymphoma. I was always glad to answer with a firm no!

Then, I woke up one night, and my shirt was soaked. Of course, my mind went straight to a place of fear. The lymphoma must be back! In the coming weeks there were even a few times I had to change the sheets in the middle of the night.

During a routine gynecological appointment, I mentioned the night sweats. The doctor said they were likely the infamous hot flashes of menopause! Night sweats of lymphoma are like menopausal symptoms. He followed by stating chemotherapy is known to put women into menopause. Wait, what? Menopause? Well, I was now fifty-one after all, but I had not even considered that as a possibility. The topic of menopause being triggered by chemotherapy had never been brought up during or after treatment.

A blood test confirmed that yes, I was in menopause. For all you women out there, we know that menopause means one thing: aging. It's a somber event to say the least. Well, for many women, it is anyway, but not for this girl! I let out a whoop of joy when they told me I was in menopause. A wave of relief washed over me. This meant the night sweats were normal.

Giving My Gynecologist a Go at the Intimacy Issue

During the exam, the doctor asked what I was feeling, as in physical sensation. As he was poking and prodding, I think he asked ten different times: "Can you feel that?" The answer was consistently no.

After the exam, he told me I should have felt the pressure he was applying. Apparently, I was in the midst of a very slow recovery from chemotherapy, and it had damaged most of the perineal nerves. It confirmed that the lack of feeling was not in my head. On the other hand, I started worrying, *What if this is permanent?*

He said, "You went through hell and back."

My body had been bombarded with chemotherapy and the side effects are numerous and far-reaching. He said it could take an indefinite amount of time for recovery of sensation. There is also a possibility the sensation may never come back. He did say that the more we try, the more it will help the area rejuvenate.

John was encouraged by the doctor's orders, naturally. The doctor also was clear; there wasn't really anything he could prescribe or recommend. Just be patient. We left with some satisfaction that at least someone had seen this before, but I wanted to be *normal*! I wanted my life back—all of it!

"Vajajay" Surgery?

Looking to exhaust every option, my oncology team suggested paying a visit to the hospital's Center for Women's Health to see a specialist. We assumed they had solutions for these sorts of problems—or so we hoped. Boy, were we wrong!

When I called to schedule, I was bound and determined to avoid being sent to the wrong person. When scheduling the appointment, I was very clear about what the problem was. The physician they were assigning me to was a specialist in uterine prolapse. Huh? I knew what this was from my medical background, and I was shocked this was where they wanted me to go. Though I insisted this was not my issue, they continued to insist he was the one who could help. So, trusting their professional judgment, I agreed.

Once we were called back to an examination room, the fiasco began. A young, wet-behind-the-ears resident proceeded to dive right into why I came. For ten minutes, I had to divulge my full cancer story and sexual issues to a man the same age as my twin sons. This subject was sensitive and embarrassing to me, and he wasn't even the doctor I came to see! It's not like we were dealing with a stubbed toe.

After I provided him with enough information to make us both blush, he left and said the doctor would be in soon. When the specialist arrived with his intern in tow, I had to go through the *entire* story again! The specialist did a pelvic exam, and after three to five minutes, we were done. I was so done.

After spilling my deepest, most personal emotional and physical problems to a resident and an experienced physician who I hoped could help me, he flat-out told me he did not even deal with sexual dysfunction issues. He even asked me why I came to see him! OMG! I was just beside myself, especially since I had taken steps to make sure that the referral was going to the right specialist.

Ultimately, to leave me with some nugget of a solution, he suggested pelvic reconstructive surgery could help. I did not think the first suggestion would be that I needed surgery, but that is what came out of his mouth. He deals in reconstructive, vaginal-related surgery for women who are having issues with urinary and fecal incontinence, pelvic organ prolapses, and other related problems. He had no idea how to help me. None. I certainly didn't fit his specialty. He wasn't even close with his "diagnosis," and he clearly did not consider what I had explained. But anything can be fixed with a knife, right?

My frustrations were twofold. First, I felt foolish for even going to the doctor with something they clearly found trivial enough to offer only a pat on the wrist. Surgery on my vagina? There had to be something more. Overwhelmingly, though, I was angry. Not simply for myself, but for cancer survivors everywhere. I've come to know that this is an exceedingly common problem, yet it doesn't get mentioned in any of the literature about surviving cancer. In a way, this instance serves as a microcosm for *all* of the collective trials, tribulations, and inconvenient truths survivors often may have to face entirely on their own.

A Liberating Experience Overseas

Breaking out of your comfort zone is scary, but it can be very healing. While visiting our son and his wife in Germany, an opportunity presented itself by way of a Roman-Irish bath and spa. There were multiple natural pools of spring water of varying temperatures. You can be scrubbed, oiled, massaged, and pampered for much of the day. Is there a catch? Yes, there is one slight catch—you must be naked! Truth be told, it was liberating! I cannot lie though; I was terribly self-conscious and apprehensive about walking around with all my surgical scars in sight, and my hair was just growing back in after chemo. I contemplated not going and just taking a walk around the town of Baden-Baden while John enjoyed his spa visit, but people were there for their own health—not to gawk and stare at us or anyone else. I took a deep breath and decided I was not going to let what happened dictate my life.

I needed to expose my scars on the outside to begin healing the scars that ran deep on the inside. That day, I shed my clothes—and the self-imposed negative perception of my body that was a formidable barrier to rekindling my relationship with John.

Intimacy Today

So, where are we with all this now? Was I wrong to search for answers and solutions for this issue so diligently? No way. I can tell you unequivocally that having the conversation as a couple openly and regularly has been critical. This process has deepened and strengthened our relationship. Intimacy is still a work in progress. Sexual health is not stand-alone issue. In fact, it is very much a part of the road to recovery, and it is an integral part of all aspects of healing, including mental, emotional, and physical well-being. One is not independent of the other. I began to experience improvement in my sexual health as the other aspects of my well-being came into balance.

In searching for answers to help our intimacy issues, I felt like I was abnormal—even perverted—for feeling so strongly about the sexual part of my life and that I was wrong to seek help. The general tone was that I should be thankful that I had survived cancer and that sexual intimacy was not something I should be concerned with. The professionals said that this was going to be the new normal. I truly felt like my womanhood was taken from me (initially by cancer and then reinforced by the medical establishment). While I do not believe the doctors were intentionally trying to diminish my concerns, it is clear sexual health for recovering survivors is not at the forefront of the issues openly addressed by the medical world.

John and I continue to be patient and talk about intimacy and continue to work through it. Like everyone else, we have our ups and downs, but our love for each other is strong—and that matters above all else. I wish I could leave you with a magic answer, but there is not one. Intimacy needs to be openly talked about.

Lessons Learned

1. Cancer, or any chronic or life-threatening illness and the treatment that goes with it, will wreak havoc on the body, including the seldom talked about internal and external reproductive organs and areas surrounding them.
2. Communicate with each other. Talk about intimacy and sex openly and often. Share what is working and what is not. Listen—without judgment.
3. Experiment! Discuss new things to try. Go to a reputable adult novelty store. Some even have staff trained to help recommend novelty products to help regain intimacy after illness. Find mutually agreeable things to try. Don't be afraid to venture a little out of your comfort zone.
4. Don't judge. The real healing may never occur if you apply pressure and blame on yourself or your partner.
5. When seeking professional help, be direct and insistent about the issues and what you need. Be prepared that you may not find the solutions you hoped for. That doesn't mean settle; instead, seek out second and third opinions.
6. You are not broken or a failure. Be kind to yourself. This can get better.
7. And, of course, if at first you don't succeed, try, try again!

CHAPTER 10B: JOHN

Neither Can I!

I Can't Believe My Family and Friends Are About to Read This!

It just came to a halt. A screeching, immediate halt. Romance, intimacy, sex—all of it.

We all know the stereotypes about men and sex and how men think about doing it all day long, wake up thinking about it, go to bed thinking about it, and think about it when we look at women. Well, we kinda do! Lucky for me that Sherri and I had kept the fires burning over the years. When cancer hit like a bomb, life changed overnight. We went from bliss to despair in the blink of an eye.

Immediacy of Cancer

So, when the immediacy of the situation suddenly exploded upon us, it didn't take me long to realize that I had no clue how to handle foregoing intimacy and physical love—or, hell, even just physical touch. I had no idea that there would be days when Sherri would not have the energy to even give a hug or that she would feel so feeble and weak that getting out of bed required physical assistance. I really had no one I could turn to for advice or guidance. There was no one to prepare me for this part of the battle as a caregiver. I am certain I never wondered about how people handled intimacy after illness. This is an important topic, yet it is clearly overlooked.

My desire had not left me, but my spouse had none, creating an internal conflict. Trying to imagine not having desire is a tough one for any man to wrap his head around. This war of conscience begins to grow in the mind: the desire for physical love versus the horrible guilt I experienced for even thinking about sex while Sherri was in a hospital bed. We cannot help how we are wired, and the situation was not going to change. I had to accept there would be no resolution to this internal conflict for some time.

The Last Time

I do not know why, because at the time I had no idea it would be the last for a while, but I vividly remember the last time we made love before Sherri was finally diagnosed and began chemo. We were headed to a concert near Pittsburgh, and I had hoped the getaway would be a great distraction from how she had been feeling of late, especially with her coughing and all. I hoped we would be able have a romantic evening.

The show was fantastic, and we did indeed make love that night. Sherri was exhausted and tired, but she wanted to—just as I did. She crashed into a deep sleep immediately after. I remember that night with great clarity. I will never be mistaken for a fortune-teller or a clairvoyant, but I somehow knew that was going to be the end of intimacy for quite some time.

Romance? Lovemaking? These became the least important things in our lives the moment the final diagnosis was handed down. Life now was about facing this demon with Sherri head-on and waging a war for her life. There was no time to worry about desires and needs. As it turned out, my sexual needs were not going to be satisfied for nearly a year.

You Can't Just Turn It Off

Some of those nights lying in bed were long and lonely. I was often alone because Sherri's coughing would be so bad that she would sleep in a spare room. And there I lay, solitary in our bed with a million thoughts running through my mind. I would ponder how she was feeling, how she was progressing, if the treatments would work, and what would happen if things went south for her—and even worse, considering what would happen if I lost her.

And, yes, I also lay there thinking about love, intimacy, and sex. If you asked me to my face, I would have to be honest. So here it is; I am baring my soul. Yes, from time to time, I satisfied myself. No one would want to admit this, and I hate the idea of my family reading this, but as they say, it is what it is.

Afterward, I felt like a piece of shit, and an overwhelming sense of guilt and selfishness would envelop me. I felt as if I had somehow cheated and put my own selfish desires over Sherri. I came to learn later that, according to a sexual health therapist, apparently it was perfectly normal to have these feelings. Since I was not the one who was ill and being treated, my body's natural drive was still intact. I suppose if this is my greatest sin from that time, I will live with it because I would never have gone the other route and sought intimacy elsewhere. Unfaithfulness never once entered my mind. I cannot imagine, even for a second, quitting on her, which is exactly what I would have been doing by being unfaithful. In the end, I am eternally grateful that our bond, and a loving marriage got us through all of this.

Sun + Sand + Sea = Love?

Off to the teal waters of the Caribbean! One day, when Sherri was resting in her hospital bed, I made the conscious decision that when we got through this, we were going to *live*. I mean, we were going to live—and live hard. I made a pact with myself that we were not going to let the grass grow under our feet. If we could handle it, we were going to travel and be active as much as possible. So, as soon as Sherri was able, I planned to take her on a getaway.

By the time we were able to travel, Sherri was walking on her own and finally growing some hair back. I made sure a bouquet of flowers was already in place in our room when we arrived. The more special I could make this, the better the odds of getting her mind off of all she had been through and refocused on living. The sound of the sea, the bright sunshine, the feel of the sand beneath her feet, and the ever-blowing trade winds were going to be the best medicine. Further, if we could get close and intimate again, that would be a serious bonus!

We were both nervous about being intimate again. I longed for it, and Sherri had no real desire. What a combination, right? The first day of the vacation, we tried to make love, but it did not go well. We just could not force this, and it would not happen overnight. She was terribly self-conscious about her body, and the whole experience was proving to be a mental and physical obstacle for her. Despite being away from home in a beautiful, tropical place at a quaint resort, this was going to require time, patience, understanding, and a whole lot of love.

We were able to have some success on that trip, but the most important thing was that Sherri was able to relax, take in the Caribbean, soak up some sun, and truly be at peace. We toured the island, tried different foods, and walked on the beach every day. This trip provided both of us some necessary healing. I did not realize as a caregiver how exhausted and emotionally spent I was from this arduous journey we had been on for so long. Seeing Sherri start to relax, laugh, and enjoy life again brought relief for me. We both began to physically unwind and find peace.

We Both Felt the Pressure

Making love is supposed to be a mutual affair. Both parties are supposed to enjoy the experience, building to a crescendo. For many people, this is what sets making love apart from just having sex. Unfortunately, because Sherri had such little sensation, oftentimes, especially early on in our efforts to regain the passion, there was a great deal of pressure on me. Having had to work so hard to help her become aroused, I was working overtime to help her feel pleasure. It became a chore. Sometimes I was unable to experience a climax as my own arousal would pass.

For a period, the thought of trying to make love again and how much work it would be often killed the arousal. This all added up to personal mental strain; consequently, I began to think maybe I had a problem, and it wasn't all Sherri. Great! Now we both are having intimacy and sexual issues. The tension grew for a while, and I think there were times when we both were ready to give up.

Fast-forward to today. We have tried many things, and in the end, it seems that *time* and *patience* were truly the remedy. And of course, love. I can smile happily today when I say we have been able to rekindle that fire. Sherri is physically in a much better place, I am mentally in a better place, and intimacy has gradually worked its way back into our lives.

Takeaways

Bringing this chapter to a close and in searching for some final words of wisdom, three come to mind instantly: love, commitment, and patience. We were then, and remain now, entirely committed to each other. Our love is what brought us through, and our love will get us through hard times that may lay ahead. When we said, "For better or for worse," we meant it. In the meantime, we try to live in the moment, be patient with one another, and know that today is a gift.

1. This is not about you—so don't make it that. Your ego needs to go away. The physiological changes your partner has experienced may make it impossible for them to enjoy sex for some time.
2. Communicate, talk about it openly, and let each other know feelings, needs, fears, etc.
3. Intimacy does not only have to be about sex; it can be a gesture, a hug, a note, or a compliment. You devalue your relationship if sex is all that matters.
4. One more time: love, commitment, and patience.
5. Tomorrow? Nothing is guaranteed. Live in the moment.

CHAPTER 11A: SHERRI

I Go Back

Triggers: A Loaded Gun

There it is … the exit for the Ohio State University Medical Campus. My stomach is in knots. Now the sign for the Medical Center Drive exit comes into view. I hate that sign.

As the exit approaches, I can see Ohio Stadium where the Buckeye football team plays. Then the James Cancer Hospital, my second home over the course of my treatment, comes into view, looming over me like a black storm cloud. As we approach for a routine oncology checkup, my mind goes into overdrive. What if they find irregularities in my blood work? What if I have a fever when they take my temperature or my O2 sats are low? I let out a cough. Oh no! My lungs—what if there are new nodules?

We check in and wait to be called back. I am quiet, and John knows to just let me be. Once I get called back, it means the appointment is almost over—and we can go home until the next one. I wonder if this institution will ever just be a place again and not the source causing a pit of fear in my stomach.

It took more than two years into recovery before there was a day when we drove by the James and I could just give it a passing glance, like any other building along the highway, without being triggered by ominous thoughts. When that finally happened, it marked a big milestone. I was moving on!

Living in Fear

For a long time, I only needed one hand to count the number of days between triggers that launched me back down the path of paranoia again. Any ache or pain immediately sent my mind to the worst-case scenario. I am a catastrophist. At a deeper level, it means I don't want to be surprised by bad news. Instead, I create the worst-case scenario in my mind before it can really happen. Cancer and all the unexpected complications caught me off guard, and my mind jumps instantly into this protective mode anytime a potential health issue occurs. Being a catastrophist is like a hypochondriac on steroids; all it does is stress me out more.

Working in the health care world as a nurse and as a massage therapist for most of my life, I have come across many people who could be classified as hypochondriacs: someone abnormally fixated on their real or imagined health issues. As a school nurse, it is surprising the number of staff members who line up at the clinic door to tell me all about their symptoms and self-diagnosed diseases. I've looked at rashes, felt lumps and bumps, and heard graphic details of GI issues. Some of these people aren't feeling good if they're not feeling bad. There was no way I was ever going to be that type of person! Then cancer happened.

Identifying the Triggers: My New Phobias

After surviving cancer, I believed I was going to be fine—but then I discovered that certain triggers made me stop on a dime. In those moments, time stands still. My fears are based upon experience. At many appointments, I went in expecting good news, but there always seemed to be another issue or more bad news. For a full year, my appointments often ended in feeling defeated.

An upcoming appointment would loom in my mind from the day it was scheduled until it was over. Those appointments would build like a storm brewing, but they were not the only triggers—not by a long shot. There is a label for every fear out there it seems. There is the typical *scanitis*, which is also called *scanxiety* (a dreadful fear of what a scan may reveal). Anytime a scan was ordered, I panicked—and worries took over my thoughts.

Hemaphobia, by definition, is an irrational fear of blood, blood tests, or any other situation where blood may be involved. Blood is not the issue. Heck, I am a nurse, for heaven's sake! But mention a blood test, and my stomach twists into a knot. Scans and blood work go hand in hand, eliciting fear. My whole mood and demeanor shift, and dark clouds loom over me. Magnify that anxiety tenfold as the long wait for test results ensues. Results that, only in my mind, are going to be bad news. The test results in the past few of years have been normal. With time, the anxiety has lessened, but it has not totally disappeared.

Technology advances have resulted in online correspondence between patient and health care providers. This has made patients more interactive in the health care system and provided them empowerment and self-advocacy, but I hate the message alerts! The alerts transport me instantly back to being the sick cancer patient, waiting for lab results, even though I know the alert is for something not even related to the cancer like a bill or appointment reminder.

Latrophobia is a legitimate fear of doctors and medical appointments. I had never experienced this before cancer. Never. Although I really like my medical team and am grateful for them, it doesn't mean I look forward to the visits, fearing the potential news they could be bearing. By the mood of my fellow cancer comrades in the waiting room before our oncology appointments, I can see we share this same fear. What does this appointment hold? Will my life continue—or do I get the news the cancer is back? Am I facing the possibility of treatments starting over again? Fortunately, my appointments of late have been more of a reunion with my oncologist and nurse practitioner.

Carcinophobia is the fear of developing cancer. Uh, yep! I've got this one also. Since I've already had cancer, now it's actually a fear of recurrence. This fear may never completely go away, but it is diminishing over time.

Common Sense: The Conqueror of Fear

Eventually, these phobias became more than I could handle, and John was at his wit's end trying to keep me calm, offering constant reassurances. I decided to tell my oncology team how the anxiety was starting to control my thoughts.

When I shared my fears with the doctor, he said something quite prophetic, which has been crucial for me to remember. Rolling off my tongue were a litany of "symptoms" I was worried about while he patiently listened.

He said, "Just because you had cancer doesn't mean you aren't human. You will still get the same typical illnesses, aches, and pains everyone else gets."

Click! The light bulb came on in my head. He was so right! Sometimes we get so wrapped up in being a cancer patient that the world revolves around the cancer merry go-round—and we forget the ride may end, and it is time to move on.

Physical and Environmental Triggers

There are many "less institutional-based" triggers that cause me to worry.

Predicting the Weather

We all have bad habits we would like to eliminate, and coughing is my Achilles' heel. My version of lymphoma (I feel as if I owned it) originated in my lungs, and a continuous cough is what got the whole ball rolling. When a stressful situation arises, such as giving a presentation at work, entering a new place, or meeting new people—anything out of my comfort zone—I start to have that nervous cough, which just feeds the fear animal.

The most fear triggering coughs are related to weather. Travel brochures don't advertise the weather in Ohio—and for good reason. Much of the year averages 50 degrees, and it is cold and damp. This sort of weather is not friendly to my lungs. My chest gets tight, and the coughing begins. Just like someone who can predict weather from arthritis in their joints, I will start to cough when a rainy weather system is rolling in. I should be used to this by now, but it takes me right back to cancer.

The logical part of my brain knows it's nothing! In fact, the pulmonary doctors were very clear with me as my treatments neared their conclusion. Since I have scar tissue in my lungs, they are more susceptible to moisture, dampness, allergens and smoke, and I am at a higher risk to contract chest colds and infections. "This is your new normal," they said. Now I hold onto the word "normal" to remind me that I am OK.

As time passes, it gets easier. Eventually, you will reach a point where you recognize the triggers that cause anxiety and implement techniques that prevent them from turning into fear or panic. Breathing and positive affirmations always seem to help me settle my mind and allow me to take control of my mindset. Here is a simple affirmation I use: "I am happy. I am healthy. I am holy." Immediately, my mind takes a pause and resets, preventing fear from taking over my thoughts.

You're Still Human

You either know now or will discover that getting older brings aches and pains. Our bodies just are not quite as spry and resilient as they used to be. My first thought when I have a bothersome ache isn't to recall what may have caused it. Nope, my mind is more like: "Oh, God, what organ is near the ache or pain? Is the cancer back but metastasized into a bigger more aggressive monster?"

After eating beets for the first time during recovery, the very next day my urine was tinged pink. My heart jumped out of my chest. Blood in the urine for a postmenopausal woman could only mean one thing: bladder or a gynecological cancer! Definitely not the case thankfully! The compound in beets that gives them their red pigment may cause the appearance of blood in urine or stool! When I remembered that I had eaten beets the night before, everything was good again.

Put on the brakes! Take a step back and think through what the real cause of your concern could be. Your nagging headache doesn't mean brain cancer; maybe you just sat staring at that computer monitor too damn long. Remember that, yes, you are human, and yes, you will get regular "noncancer" people issues.

Lessons Learned

At some point, a line had to be drawn in the sand. Living in fear is not who I am and not who I want to be. If this pattern had continued, that means cancer defines me and is no longer something that just happened to me. The time had come to face my fears. Here are some simple steps that were helpful:

1. Remember, you are still human.
2. Worrying never solves anything—and 98 percent of the things we worry about never happen. Stop, take a deep breath, and remember this.
3. Positive thinking. The National Science Foundation found we have upwards of sixty thousand thoughts per day, and 95 percent of them are the exact same thoughts, day after day. And 80 percent of those thoughts are negative. The mind is like a muscle, and it

takes practice to reset the default button to positive. You *will* need to work hard at this.

4. Find a positive affirmation or mantra that speaks to you. It should be short and easy to remember: Right now, things are good! Don't look to the future or live in the past. Be in the here and now. You may need to say your mantra ten times a day or a thousand times. Just keep doing it—and then notice how your mind shifts to a calmer state. This calm state will eventually be the norm.

5. Read. I read many self-help books. I have not found a single book that had all the answers. Taking bits and pieces from a variety of resources allowed me to put together a tool kit that was specific to my needs. Some things you read will instantly resonate with you, and others may leave you scratching your head. Listen to your own inner voice. You will find what reverberates with you.

6. Find your support peeps. Find that posse of friends who make you smile and laugh and are there for you. Even talking to others who shared the cancer experience can be immensely helpful. Anytime I cross paths with a fellow survivor, the conversation inevitably leads to us sharing and finding commonalities in our experiences.

7. Acceptance. At the end of the day, I know I suffer from a form of PTSD. Cancer is trauma. It wasn't until I accepted this that I could acknowledge the triggers and let them go. Any little thing can set off a flood of emotions. Knowing that the trigger is just that—a trigger and no more—is a victory.

CHAPTER 11B: JOHN

A Voice of Reason

Disarming the Triggers

Sherri's eyes would get as big as saucers when she had a blood draw, scan, or test. Looking at her was like staring into the barrel of a loaded gun, the trigger cocked. *How am I going to disarm her in such an anxious state?* In my ongoing role as caregiver, this continues to be a challenge. My responses and actions are not centered on some scientific psychological study. They are based on consistency and staying the course—no matter how tiresome it all gets.

No, You Do Not Have Brain Cancer

Memory issues have plagued Sherri since recovery began; it is a living hell at times with the triggered response of worry that she will develop brain cancer, Alzheimer's, or dementia. Most of this paranoia can be credited to the seed a neurologist planted saying she had brain cancer. On a CT scan, he saw two spots and stated confidently that they were malignant. There was no evidence that the cancer had crossed the blood-brain barrier. Hadn't she been through enough already without adding this sort of speculation? God knows she had enough spinal taps to fill a gallon bottle. Add all that to the ever-present struggle with memory, and it is not difficult to understand the fear Sherri battles in her mind. That "seed" he planted ended up being a fungal infection—not cancer—but the damage was done.

This is where my support and having a consistent voice of reason becomes critical. She looks to me for confirmation that she is fine and that what she is experiencing is normal, just part of the ongoing effects of chemo brain. We need one of the British WWII posters plastered to the main wall of our home: "Keep calm and carry on." Sherri sometimes believes the occurrences and lapses in recall are becoming more frequent, but in reality, they are not. Sometimes I just need to give her a gentle reminder that being tired after a long day is the reason she may struggle with memory or finding the right words.

Holding My Tongue

I often ponder if she will ever fully get over her fears and accept some of these new realities. No one can blame her; anyone would struggle with all this. Nevertheless, there are those days when I privately think, *Good God, not again*, when she gets upset and fearful. Sometimes it gets tiresome having to be Mr. Support and Mr. Reassurance all the time. It's like, "Hey, for once, can we not worry about you getting cancer again and just relax?" Sounds horribly cruel, and it would be if I voiced it. I would never voice these feelings. It is certainly normal for you as a caregiver to feel such emotion. But never act on it. Remember, your loved one went through hell and lives in a world where relapse is a legitimate concern.

When she has those chemo moments, I also wonder if she will finally reach a point where she says, "Enough of this! There is nothing wrong with me!" I would love to see her flip her mindset to this sort of aggressive confidence. Sherri becomes overwhelmed with it all every now and then, sometimes to the point of tears. In those moments, what I do and how I respond can make all the difference in the world. Here is an example:

Surprisingly, reading a menu can be quite difficult. When Sherri was about eight months out from her final treatment, we took a long weekend and buzzed down to just south of Atlanta to see Zac Brown Band in a small, intimate concert. Some other friends from Ohio came down for the event as well. We all met up for breakfast at a local greasy spoon. Sherri was still in early stages of recovery, and her confidence was low. Now, completely out of her comfort zone, we were in a public setting, eating with others, and she was terribly worried about just having a normal, relaxed conversation, fearing she would stumble over words. Knowing she was worried and nervous, I remained on guard in and in a protective mode.

Once we were seated, the server brought us menus—and that is when the bottom fell out. The menu was huge; they pretty much offered every type of food under the sun. Sherri started paging through and was staring at the menu as if it were in a foreign language. I glanced over and thought,

Oh no, her menu is upside down! She was in such a state of overwhelming panic that she didn't notice.

As a teacher, I am acutely aware of the struggle some students have with dyslexia. This was different; Sherri was not even seeing the words. The panic seemingly blinded her. We discreetly flipped the menu the right way, and I began to talk her through the different sections and help her calm down so she could choose a meal she would like.

The server kept coming back and asking if we were ready to order. Luckily, our company was a chatty bunch, and no one was ready. Still, Sherri had no idea what she wanted. I knew the words were scrambling in front of her very eyes, and she was shedding tears. Everyone saw it. And that magnified the whole event. Sherri was beyond agitated and frustrated.

Slowly, calmly, and carefully, I was able to settle her down, and we placed an order that she seemed happy with. Off she went to the restroom to compose herself. This allowed me to explain to the group what she had been experiencing. Luckily, both couples had some exposure to cancer in their families, and they were truly kind, sympathetic, and extremely understanding.

Keep Calm

In the midst of the menu incident, I knew remaining discreet and calm was the most important thing to do. I became something of a "whisperer", just speaking in a quiet, relaxing voice that only she could hear. It is so important to play the role of a comforting warm blanket in those moments, being able to envelop her in safety and security.

Prove it!

A primary rule in my classes as a teacher is that any argument or position must be substantiated with evidence. The evidence must come from legitimate, reliable, and unbiased sources—just your basic rules of argumentative writing and discussion. Never realizing how much I would have to rely on this with Sherri, she took me to task literally dozens of times—and she still does on some occasions—by making me verify the things her doctors say.

From the start of Sherri's battle with cancer, I took notes and documented every visit. Though they were originally meant as a guide for me to help care for Sherri during treatment, during recovery, they became a tool to use to reassure her of what to expect in recovery. You'll see how valuable tool they could be.

Yes, They Did Say This Is Your New Normal

As you may have gleaned from reading Sherri's triggers, even the slightest cough can set her mind running. "Chicken Little" thinking the sky is falling, but there is nothing wrong with her. Trying to convince her of this is a major hurdle. Logic does kick in because she knows she is fine and should have nothing to worry about. However, the sum of her experiences weighs heavily and often negates logic. Sometimes it is as if she wills herself to cough.

In those moments, we revisit the last bronchoscopy she had near the end of treatment. They were wheeling Sherri down the hall to a recovery room since she was groggy from the procedure. They had me join the parade of staff to her room, and the pulmonologist explained everything quite clearly along the way. I took damn good notes. He found her bronchial passageways to be wide-open, almost dilated. In addition, there was a great deal of scar tissue all through the lungs. The scar tissue was the result of the chemo destroying the lymphoma granulation. This was no surprise to him as he stated that chemotherapy, lifesaving though it is, can cause a lot of permanent changes and damage.

Now, here is the key part, which I always reiterate to Sherri when she is uptight and upset about a cough: "The doctor was clear as crystal when he said these bronchial airways will remain dilated and, combined with the scar tissue, he said you will always be more susceptible to coughing when the air is damp or you inhale anything beyond normal air, like dust or exhaust or anything like that." Jokingly, I've considered painting these words on the ceiling of our bedroom so she will see it every day! The pulmonologist emphasized these points to me, and the oncologist *and* the infectious disease doctor confirmed it. This is your "new normal." She never remembers hearing any of that, so I am always there, ready to remind her that she is A-OK. When I see her put a hand to her chest and cough, it actually triggers me to give her the weather report: "Yes, honey, it is going to rain." So, caregivers, take good notes! Lesson over.

Yes, You Should Try That

These damn triggers are fewer now, but they get in the way of Sherri living her best life. Sometimes the smallest triggers come in rapid succession. Sherri has had moments when a chain reaction is started, and one little trigger sets the ball in motion. Things deteriorate quickly when she begins to play out scenarios in her mind. A cough starts in, and she soon remembers she had a small headache earlier. The ball is rolling faster now as she begins contemplating that the cancer is back in her lungs *and* her brain. In a matter of time, she will have herself in hospice and telling me I should find someone else when she is gone. I kid you not. But who can blame her? Once something bad happens, isn't it normal to wonder if it will happen again? Don't people who have been bitten by dogs at an early age develop a fear of dogs that can last a lifetime? When she begins to experience consistent triggers, it is time for a distraction.

Getting involved helps keep her mind from worrying about things that could, but aren't, happening. New activities provide distractions from the ghosts of fear that haunt her. Sherri loves to discover new things, including painting, drawing, and meditation. The key is for her to be involved and be a normal functioning adult—just like anyone else. These new activities fill her life with things she enjoys rather than remnants of cancer.

Playing the role of encourager is your role as caregiver. The goal is for your loved one to get back into the things they enjoy and, more importantly, challenge their minds and grow. So, besides going to work and doing a fitness routine, if I cannot find Sherri, chances are she is busy doing something! As a matter of fact, as I sit here and type this segment, Sherri is painting at the kitchen table and singing along to some of her favorite songs. You go, girl!

Takeaways: "Un-triggering" Your Warrior

1. Stay calm. Always.
2. Listen. Let them talk, vent, and express their fears. Don't butt in. Stealing from one of Sherri's lessons learned: "Listen to respond— not just to react."

3. Once you have listened, pause—and then rely on what you know and refer to what the experts have told you. Use those notes or even contact the doctors to clarify if needed. The goal here is reassurance and peace of mind.

4. Reassure, reassure, reassure, but with evidence. Be that safe place your loved one goes to when they just need to feel like things are OK, and you can literally support that all is fine.

5. Encourage independence to grow, learn, and challenge themselves. Join in and share those experiences when it serves the purpose—even if it is just to show support. Inevitably, you will find new interests together and discover things to talk about besides living in the past. Grow together.

6. Remember, no matter how annoyed you may get with these groundless triggers, your loved one is anxious and frightened. This ain't about you! Their minds take them to a dark place. You must be the light. For them, the symptoms and thoughts are real. Respect that. Their perception is their reality.

7. Know when to step in and when not to. Sometimes, it's best to just give them space.

8. Did I mention *listening* to them?

CHAPTER 12: SHERRI

The Healing Highway

A Holistic Approach

I have healed, and I have moved on—or at the very least, I *am* moving on.

Although I don't believe we are ever entirely healed from something like cancer, it is an evolutionary process, and it *does* get easier. It is a long journey on a winding highway with twists and turns to navigate. If we are lucky, the struggle can lead us in a new, different, and awesome direction. Life is evolving, and my path is slowly and gradually taking shape! There will be both good days and bad days, but I am determined to make the most of every day.

As a nurse for more than thirty years, even though much of it has not been on the front lines in a hospital, I still have seen a lot of advancements in all areas. For instance, the advances in science have led to groundbreaking medications. It seems like every day, a new drug has been approved by the FDA to help combat health issues like COPD, diabetes, or heart disease. Science saved my life, but I also experienced many problems because of the science and chemistry used to annihilate the cancer. A miracle drug or chemical solved one problem, but it created many more. Those new side effect issues were then treated and curbed with other drugs. There were even side effects for those. There is no finger-pointing here! Modern medicine was necessary, and I followed the doctors' orders.

As the gap between medical appointments widened and reliance on my medical team lessened, I developed a strong curiosity and desire to explore more holistic options that might help me deal with minor symptoms and issues when they arose.

The simple modality of diffusing essential oils during chemotherapy helped me find relief for nausea, insomnia, and anxiety without the use of prescription medication that had originally been prescribed to me. The questions were simple: Are there safe ways to support my body without pharmaceuticals? How can I decrease the need to constantly contact the doctor for minor issues? There are some simple things out there that are under our complete control, and they can help make a difference in maintaining good health.

What Is a Naturopathic Doctor?

Do I call the doctor or not? For the first two years out of treatment, the triggers that sparked my anxieties often brought the urge to call my oncology team. They were, after all, my security blanket. Somehow, I needed to get out in front of my health.

While researching holistic health options, I learned all I could about naturopathic medicine. I decided it was yet another path for me to try. Naturopathic medicine has a long history, much of it brought to the United States from different parts of the world, as well as from Native American practices. Naturally, being Miss Curious, I needed to explore this option. I found a practitioner and booked a visit. There are many people who make assertions outside their scope of practice and make false claims with the intent of draining your wallet, which is why researching in advance was so important.

My goal in seeing a naturopathic doctor was to look at options that would help support my immune system. As a medical professional, I felt it was important to communicate with my medical team about the alternatives I was investigating. Taking prescription medications along with certain supplements can be contraindicated—so make sure all parties involved in your care are aware of what the others are doing.

The naturopath recommended a couple of supplements to help strengthen my overall immune system—not as a replacement for anything I had already been prescribed. Supplements are big business. All retailers— whether a big box store, online, or health food store—claim they have the purest and best supplements available, but none of these herbal, all-natural supplements are regulated by the FDA. People in desperate situations are so vulnerable to these lofty promises and grab onto supplements like a lifeline thrown to them as they drown. I felt safe and confident in the naturopathic doctor over time and knew she was reputable. For one, she only made a couple of affordable suggestions and did not try to sell me a special brand or blend she had created. Two, she made no claims about curing anything. She only supported good health practices. Finally, she didn't want me to keep coming back repeatedly.

In the end, it was a good decision for me. I saw her a few times over the course of a year, and I saw improvements in my overall health as a result of her simple, holistic suggestions. Skeptics would say I would have seen these improvements anyway, but the true answer is we can only find it within.

Taking the Leap to a Plant-based Life

John loves ribs, and actually all meat as a rule, but when the cancer struck, our eyes were opened wide about the power and value of a plant-based diet. During treatment, we focused on eating healthy as well as careful food preparation to protect my immunosuppressed body. Before being discharged entirely from cancer treatment, the James Survivorship program set us up with a knowledgeable dietitian and a great cookbook. They also had hands-on cooking classes that allowed us to cook, learn, and share the meal with other cancer patients and their caregivers. Seek out programs like this!

The learning was wonderful, but the camaraderie with others who shared our story was indescribable. The meal-preparation protocols they gave us for preparing food during chemotherapy had been lifted, but there was no way were we going back to a typical diet that was high in fat and cholesterol. John and I both agreed that this was the time to make a commitment. We embraced the plant-based diet we learned in those classes. Since then, we have immersed ourselves in plant-based cookbooks, particularly those that pull recipes from areas of the world where studies have shown people are living longer, healthier, more active lives.

We saw changes to our bodies, and our energy levels soared as we removed unhealthy fats and processed foods. We focused on a diet primarily of vegetables, fruit, and nonmeat proteins. Smoothies and juicing are part of our weekly meal prep.

While I may make a plant-based diet sound fantastic, it takes work to prepare a meal. Fresh, organic foods do not have a long shelf life, and there are more frequent grocery trips. Though it would be easier to make a box of mac and cheese or go to a fast-food drive-through, I am able to look beyond the immediate gratification and see the long-term effects of our diet choices. Do we indulge in a treat now and then? Sure. Whether that be ice cream or even a burger, sometimes making certain foods not forbidden is okay. An occasional indulgence makes the plant-based lifestyle easier to follow. There is no way we can go to a wings place—and all John orders is a salad!

Take baby steps if you decide this route is for you. Perhaps eliminate meat one day a week at first or even one meal a week—and then build from that. Explore recipes on the internet; you will be amazed at the options, and in many cases, if you had not prepared the food yourself, you would not even know there is no meat in the dish! We made the right decision for us.

A healthier diet and increased energy have allowed me to be more involved in a variety of activities without getting worn down. We are sold. I recommend thorough research before you dive into a vegan or vegetarian lifestyle. If you have kids, this could be a real challenge. Having a partner on this journey has made it doable. It is daunting, and the expenses can add up if you have to cook two different meals every night to please all tastes. Even if your family is committed, you still need to do your homework. Making sure you are getting vitamins and nutrients is easy in a vegan world, but proteins are another story. I hope you like beans!

Oils and Aroma: Fighting Dependency

You have a pretty good idea of how finding natural solutions was important for me. Using them at first to curb nausea and anxiety, essential oils became a reliable, safe option for mood management.

When I was in treatment, so many different medications were prescribed. Of course, there were the chemotherapy cocktails dripping slowly into my body for one hundred consecutive hours every three weeks, but that was only the tip of the iceberg because there was a mountain of side effects that required other medications to be prescribed. I had medications for nausea, sleep, to make me poop, or to stop me from pooping! Antibiotics, antifungals, and antivirals were all being administered—sometimes simultaneously. Let's not forget medications for acid reflux and preventing ulcers! Finally, there were the opioids. The focus in treatment is beating the disease, as it should be. Getting prescribed myriad medications to solve the side effects is standard. As patients, we aren't always instructed how to manage these "as-needed" medications. Often, through no one's fault, instead of taking them only as needed, they become part of our regular daily medication regimen. An utter lack of knowledge can lead to misuse and cause unwelcome side effects or even dependence.

As a chemotherapy patient, I was not allowed to take acetaminophen or ibuprofen because it affected the lab results, which were being closely monitored all through treatment. For pain, I was prescribed an opioid. These pain meds were the hardest to quit. What initially started out as a half a tablet had grown into taking two tablets in order to get the same relief. At home, in recovery and not even in physical pain, I took the pills just for the mellow, relaxed, "no worries" state of mind they allowed me to live in. In my mind, I knew I needed to stop.

That first night not taking a pain medication to aid my sleep was difficult. I was up almost all night. No matter how bad I wanted to take a sleeping pill or pain medication, the choice was clear. I was at a crucial turning point, a fork in the road. Dependency is real, and if I took a pill that night, I would find myself heading down the path to addiction. I resisted the urge that night and the nights that followed. In time, I felt alive again. I sought other ways to help my mood and body. At that point, essential oils and aromatherapy became a regular part of my life.

"Butt" No, I Do Not Need Surgery!

During the final long stay in the hospital, I was no longer able to be active and walk the halls. As a result of all the bed rest, weight loss, and atrophy, I developed a "bony butt," which left my tailbone sore and swollen. At home, my physical activity was limited, forcing me to sit a lot, which caused my tailbone to be even more sore and tender. I could barely sit at all anymore. Becoming intolerable, it was off to another doctor!

This doctor said the only option was a surgical procedure to shave the tailbone. Surgery? No way was I going under the knife for my tailbone! Not even a thought was given to other options. The pain had become unbearable to the point where being on my side or standing offered the only relief.

John and I started brainstorming and seeking alternatives. The thought of a close friend who was a chiropractor came to mind. After one treatment—yes, just one—I could sit again without excruciating pain. He found that my sacrum needed to be adjusted since the long bed rest had caused a misalignment. After just three treatments, it was back to normal. No surgery. No medications. Neither a scalpel nor a pill was required to solve this problem. The success of the chiropractic treatment only strengthened my resolve to incorporate less invasive options instead of jumping immediately into the hamster wheel of drugs, doctor consults, and procedures.

Scar Tissue: Ouch!

Nine scars marked the trunk of my body. There was the emergency surgery scar, running midline from the sternum to below the belly button. Then there is the spleen removal scar. And who could forget "Betty Poop" and the scar where the colostomy bag had been? Several others were from biopsies and a chest tube as well. The scars caused a ripple effect on the underlying musculature and fascia. When an area of persistent pain began in my abdomen, per my usual routine, I worried and contacted the doctor. The doctor, as part of the usual routine, was going to order a CT scan.

Instead, I explored a different option that I was very familiar with: massage therapy. I wanted to explore a route that specializes in muscles and fascia to see if it could help rather than jumping into the world of scans and doctor visits. If I'd had a scan, and it didn't show an issue, the next step would have been seeing another specialist, perhaps a GI doctor, who would order more tests and probably medications. On and on goes the hamster wheel. Tests and my mental state do not jibe well.

After a couple of massage sessions that focused on the fascia and scar tissue, all the pain was eliminated. The CT scan was canceled, and my belief in complementary therapies was reaffirmed and further strengthened.

Lessons Learned

1. Above all else, do your own research! This cannot be stressed enough.
2. Find your path. My healing required finding a place where Western and Eastern medicine could coexist in my life. While I cannot recommend any of this to you, I can only share my experiences, things that helped me, and at least let you know that it may be

possible for you to find a path and incorporate a few natural options that are right for you.

3. Always consult your medical team. Your doctors have been caring for you and are most aware of potential interactions, side effects, and complications if you start adding supplements to your current medical regimen. Visiting a naturopathic doctor helped bring my mind and body back in balance. It certainly wasn't all her doing; I played a large role in seizing my life and health back.

4. Doctors will usually stay inside their wheelhouse. They are experts in their field of study, but when issues come up outside of their field, they have to live in the world they know. Not all doctors will refer or consult with other more appropriate specialists. A surgeon will look to a surgical solution, and another specialist may look to scans or other invasive procedures. And while those may end up being the solution you need, just make sure! For me, chiropractic for my tailbone and massage for my scar pain prevented me from needless surgery and another CT scan.

5. Fix your diet. Disease, particularly cancer, feeds off inflammation. Certain foods cause inflammation. A vegan option has been working for John and me, but it is not the end-all. A balanced diet is the goal. This is not about fad diets; it is about changing your life habits for the better.

6. Essential oils were a viable option that helped with typical real-life issues like sleep, anxiety, pain, and replacing harsh chemical cleaners with safer noncarcinogenic alternatives. Beware, there is a whole world out there of essential oil peddlers making dangerous claims. Consult your doctor before trying any essential oil because they could interact with a medication you are taking or a health condition.

7. Take charge of *you*! The feeling of empowerment I experienced while grabbing hold of my recovery was invigorating. You can simply survive—or you can thrive. Wherever you are in your battle, the time is always right to take control and live again.

CHAPTER 13A: SHERRI

Well-Involved versus Well-being

I Am Not Sick Anymore! But, Who Am I Now?

This is the million-dollar question we're all asking the day we get discharged from treatment. But know this: I am enjoying the journey of discovering the new version of me. My journey down Survivor Road began mostly out of the desperation of wanting to get back my old self and re-discover my old life after beating cancer.

Desperate to move on, my motto was "Charge forward!" Getting more involved would prove that cancer and sickness were no more; people would see "Sherri" and not the "cancer girl." Getting more involved was also a way to forget the past year. Little did I know, the "all-in" theory would backfire. Trying to forget what happened by diving into many activities was not the right approach. Acknowledging and incorporating the lessons that cancer has taught me is vital to balanced healing.

Every part of my being was impacted by the cancer diagnosis, treatments, complications, and side effects; my entire well-being was completely off. Everyone wants to address the physical problems; in fact, treating the physical symptoms was the primary focus during treatment. What about the mental, emotional, social, and spiritual parts of me? I was a wreck. It was not until I realized the complexity of the intertwining components that must be balanced to have a strong well-being, and addressing each one, that well-rounded healing could begin.

The Components of a Balanced Well-Being

I tried everything—almost all at once. This was a mistake. I did not comprehend how it would take time to make all the interconnected pieces of the "me" puzzle fit back together again. So, I asked, "What are the various parts of a balanced well-being?" I settled on six key areas that I needed to address. To fully heal, I needed all six components to be functioning in harmony and balance. They are all interconnected.

Here are some of my successes and failures, put in the context of these six components of well-being, to help you better understand how you can plug in your own endeavors and balance your own life. In the end, we are all on that journey to the other side of recovery in search of the answer to the big question: "Who am I now?"

Physical

The physical aspect was in my comfort zone since exercise had been a big part of my past. This is not complicated. We get one body in this life and must take care of it. This implies maintaining its condition through exercise, nutrition, cleanliness, and hydration. Bad habits that conflict with good health are hard to break. While no one is perfect, eliminating those harmful habits can prevent possibly dangerous health problems down the road. Then there is rest: the final piece. Science has proven that the body heals, recovers, and rejuvenates best when we provide adequate rest and recovery.

Mental

An idle mind is a deteriorating mind. Some say the brain is a muscle. Muscles need to be strengthened. We never stop learning, and growth is a natural part of the brain. Exercise that mind! Continue to read, learn, solve, and challenge your mind in various ways. For myself, the mental and physical became disconnected because of cancer and chemo. Only dedicated and concentrated exercise and activity for both mind and body helped them realign.

The Emotional

Often overlooked is the importance of understanding how emotions play such a vital role in well-being. We won't skip our morning jog, and we may eat our salads and drink our smoothies, but when we are stressed, such as at work, we push it aside. What we should be doing is taking a short walk to reset. One of the most critical pieces of emotional support is self-care. Relaxation and stress reduction go a long way to keeping our emotions steady and tempered. Embracing meditation and learning acceptance can pave the way for long-term healing.

Social

As members of the human race, we are indeed social beings. Being able to relate and connect with others is core to a healthy well-being. A strong nucleus of trusted and supportive friends gives us confidence, reassurance, and a sense of belonging. We are often quite isolated during treatment, making it difficult to reintegrate with others. It is easy to feel safe and comfortable in a little bubble at home. Interacting with people again may not feel quite natural at first and may cause apprehension. However, involvement in a social network adds to our own self-worth and satisfies the human need to belong.

Spiritual

Such an integral and personal part of our lives is our own spirituality. Faith and religion are the first things that comes to mind. Spirituality is as unique as the individual. Many find their spiritual balance in some aspect of their lives. Perhaps it is a cherished hobby or communing with nature. Whatever your spiritual level, feed it and nourish it as part of balancing your well-being.

Environmental

This component is all things to all people. For some, it could be their professional and financial lives or the roles they play at their companies or businesses. For others, it could mean how they interact with their own environments and the earth. It includes the ability to meet basic human needs of shelter, food, and medical care. Our environmental well-being promotes our abilities to interact in our personal spaces.

My Efforts Created Imbalance...

Arts and Crafts, Anyone? Let's Paint a Picture!

This posttreatment recovery was a time of self-discovery, and I jumped into the deep end with both feet. A lifelong dream has been to learn to draw and paint, and I enrolled in a weekly art class. The first night of class, two things were instantly apparent: first, the term "beginner" on the sign-up sheet meant nothing, and second, my brain and hand were speaking different languages. I was trying to make a circle not look like a car tire that went flat, and these DaVincis were adding various elements of shading and dimension, proudly showing off their "beginner" skills. Drawing however, was a great activity to engage my mind and try to reignite my fine motor skills. Unfortunately, it just never felt like art was being created, and instead of enjoying classes, I was consumed with comparing my lack of ability to everyone else's talent, destroying any shred of self-confidence.

The classes did more emotional harm than good. There is no question that the mental and physical aspects of my well-being could have greatly benefitted, but because I was still in a weakened emotional state, I could not handle the failure. In no way was I prepared emotionally for how much my mental and physical components had been depleted. I desperately wanted to be the old confident me. I took a pause from art classes, and before enrolling again, I needed to accept that I would never be a van Gogh—or even as good as the person sitting next to me. And you know what? That is OK.

Sew: A Needle Pulling Thread

When hospitalized for treatment at the James, volunteers rolled carts around the floors that were full of "gifts" donated for patients. Lip balms, hand lotions, and magazines were always a surprise, and I just loved when the cart came around. It lifted my spirits so much!

To give back, I began sewing little tissue holders. I filled them with tissues and dropped them off at the James to be added to the cart for others going through treatment. Positive vibes filled me while making these, and I found this very healing and empowering, both emotionally and spiritually. Even though it was a small gesture, there was a real purpose to this. The idea that I could help others motivated me to work through the challenges of problem-solving, fine motor skills, and coordination. I wasn't giving up because this was for someone else who was walking the path I had once been on.

The Garden of Hope

Many treatment centers and communities have an ever-expanding offering of classes and activities for cancer survivors and caregivers to engage in.

We found the "Garden of Hope" and interactive cooking classes through the hospital offerings. Along with going to the garden to pick fresh organic vegetables, we learned how to use them in fresh, healthy dishes. We were fully on board and into transforming our diet to one based on plants and whole organic foods. The classes were great! We cooked, ate, and communed with others in our cancer community. We shared a meal that was prepared with health and wellness in mind. Since everyone in the class had the common bond of cancer, the conversations were full of support and sharing. Knowing I am part of a community and not alone is as fulfilling as a healthy meal. These activities really boosted the social and environmental components of my well-being along with, of course, the physical.

There's an Oil for That

Needing to take back some control of my life, it became my goal to become less reliant on pharmaceuticals for symptom management. As you read earlier, I cautiously decided to explore essential oils. The nurse in me wanted to be knowledgeable about how to safely use them and not rely on a lot of the unsafe and irresponsible claims made by people on the internet.

The best way to do this was to become a certified aromatherapist. Taking classes and immersing myself in learning and growing really exercised my brain, especially my memory. Now I am making my own decisions about what essential oils would best support healing and manage symptoms based on scientific research. I was taking charge of me! Learning something new strengthens mental functioning. For me, it was seeking new knowledge and a better understanding of safer ways to maintain good health.

I Got a Rock

In my ongoing search for positive energy and health, I began reading up on the healing power of crystals and stones. This would serve well to balance the environmental component of my well-being, connecting me with the earth and its healing properties. The theory is that crystals will promote physical, emotional, and spiritual well-being. The earth and the elements are a natural part of our lives, and they indeed have a role to play in our well-being. Crystals are said to interact with our chakras in a positive way, helping to open them up and create free-flowing energy. Chakras are the body's energy fields. Crystals can be carried in a pocket, worn as a piece of jewelry, or used to decorate a home. Try it—and you may be surprised at the energy you experience. Even though there is no solid science on the healing powers of crystals, I believe they help promote a positive mindset and outlook. I've got rocks in my pockets, but I am happy!

Do I Need Counseling?

In the search for mental balance and emotional stability, I saw three counselors over the course of my illness and recovery. Each counselor was unique, and they all had different styles. It is important to be aware of the many different types of counseling. Therapists often form their practices around the theories they believe in or their foundational training. A counselor who is successful for one person may not be right for another. It's like trying to find the perfect partner; sometimes you need to go on many dates to find Mr. or Mrs. Right. If you find therapy isn't working for you, tell your therapist. They may have other options—or perhaps you would connect better with a different therapist.

All the talk in the world was not going to suddenly make a light bulb go off in my head or a voice say, "Yes, Sherri, by God, you are healed." Healing had to come from inside, and no one else could do it for me. Though I doubted it early on, I would eventually learn to cope with these new emotions in this post-cancer world I was trying to navigate. Over time, I came to realize that I was tired of talking about my story repeatedly. My cancer story was starting to define me. By the end of my last session with a therapist, she was sharing the issues she was dealing with in her own personal life; it felt like our roles had switched! Wow. Was I counseling the counselor now? This was a sign to me that I was finally on the right track!

Let's Try Group Therapy

Support groups can be extremely helpful for people and often provide a lifeline to surviving a traumatic injury, overcoming a disease, and being a caregiver. I needed to reconnect with people, and this, if it went well, could provide an opportunity for improving my emotional and social well-being. There are support groups for everything, and lymphoma is no exception.

My experience with a group I attended was that some of the people in the group really weren't ready to move on, and they lived in a fear they couldn't escape. All too aware of such fear myself, the support group for me was emotionally draining. I found myself more upset after attending. Instead of finding strength and help, my heart was heavy and depressed. This experience simply did not provide what I was looking for. Socially, I was hoping for a real connection to others, but it pulled me emotionally back into the cancer. Not going back was the right move for me; others in the group went back month after month and found the help they needed. We have commonalities in the cancer journey, but we are unique. A one-size-fits-all mentality doesn't work in cancer treatment or recovery. Try a support group and make your own decision. Shop around until you find one that fits you. When it works, it will be like finding a group of friends you just hit it off with. You will know these are your peeps. Support groups can be amazing, provide a sense of community, and help you not feel so alone.

My Attempts at Spiritual Growth

We all have our own versions of God. John and I are Catholic. We attend Mass regularly and love the spiritual food of our faith. For me, attending church is based on rituals. In this quest, I was looking to discover more of my inner spirituality and a personal connection with my higher power. Up for trying anything on this spiritual quest, we attended a shaman meditation to discover my "spirit animal" (no, not Harry Potter summoning his "patronus" animal), attended a chanting at a oneness blessing session, and even experienced lying on mats while Tibetan singing bowls filled our chakras. Was my spiritual quest satisfied? No, but I kept trying and seeking new experiences. Some experiences were hits, and some were misses, but each gave me a deeper glimpse inside myself and who I was evolving into.

A Quite Different Medicine

An "Ayurveda" class was offered at my yoga studio. John did a double take and said, "Wait, what? You're taking a class called 'Hey, Your Veda.' What the hell is that?" The practice is based on the belief that health and wellness depend on a harmonious balance between the mind, body, and spirit. Well, boom! That was exactly what I was searching for! It could be my answer as I looked to center myself and gain real balance in my well-being. According to Ayurveda, people will live their lives, including all the aspects of nutrition, exercise, career, and how they handle situations, based on their "Dosha" (body type). While several of the theories were interesting, the amount of time required to practice the lessons weighed me down and became a real source of stress because I was involved in so many things.

A Different Approach and the One That Made All the Difference

Reiki is a form of energy work, a way to balance the body's energy, enabling a person to release things they may be holding onto: fear, anger, the past, or even thoughts stored in the subconscious. Reiki is quite grounding and realigns the chakras; it has helped me overcome many of the fears raging in my heart and mind. It is difficult to explain, but in essence, it is a hands-on energy technique and not a physical massage. As a wellness coordinator for a small hospital, I used Reiki and healing touch on the oncology patients to help them relax during treatments. Luckily, I found an amazing practitioner, and the sessions helped me finally start to release the layers of doubt, anger, and fear I was holding onto throughout the cancer diagnosis, treatment, and recovery. It is not the easiest thing to describe, but in my sessions, I felt a darkness release from my heart and a tremendous weight lifted off my body. The sky seemed brighter, and my entire outlook on the future started coming into focus. Accepting the new version of me was a major part of this new awareness.

"Om"

If you are looking to create balance, meditation could provide what you need. Meditation enabled me to get into my own mind in order to get *out* of my own mind. We get into our own head way too often, and we can be our own worst enemies at times. A regular meditation practice helps break the pattern of negative self-talk and self-doubt. Meditation also helps release what is not serving us anymore. Often, it is a fear or a frustration-based thought that plants a negative seed in our minds and tries to grow like a bad weed. Improving my emotional stability meant recognizing the things that create fear, panic, and anxiety.

Meditation takes many forms. Whether it is sitting cross-legged in what many typically think of as a meditation pose or simply walking in a forest or on a beach, there is no right or wrong way to do it. What is important is just doing it. The goal is to quiet your chattering "monkey mind." People worry about thoughts entering their minds during meditation, and it stresses them. No one can make their mind free of thoughts, but people who find meditation helpful have learned to accept the thoughts that come into their mind and just allow the thoughts to float away as a cloud does in the sky. How long should you meditate? There is no time requirement; someone new to trying meditation may only calm their mind for a minute at the most. With consistent practice, perhaps the next time, that one minute can become two or three!

Is it working? You will not know if it is working while you are meditating. The realization may come one day when you react calmly to a situation or find things that used to make you upset do not anymore. That is when you'll know. There are a lot of guided meditation apps. You can even choose a theme that speaks to you.

From Patient to Practitioner

Massage therapy and Reiki were so helpful to my healing that I decided to start seeing clients again as a massage therapist! Yes, I was ready to use my passion for wellness and to help others. I realized how much I missed that part of my life. When I practiced massage therapy full-time, I was positively impacting others. Massage therapy has brought relief to those suffering from chronic pain, headaches, and many other symptoms that keep people from living life to its fullest. And as my healing progressed, I was getting a strong urge and desire to rekindle those skills and practice again.

Find Your Own Way to Journal

Starting a gratitude journal can be quite helpful. At first, I tried a daily entry, writing down three things I was thankful for. On particularly stressful days, just being able to breathe will be on my list. But carrying around or accessing a journal every day was not a passion for me, and I found myself missing and skipping days in the gratitude journal, which caused even more stress! Seriously? I mean the whole point was to focus on positivity and not to create stress. However, if it becomes a daily dread, then it is time to find something else! Now, instead of journaling every day, I do it once each week. I write down something good that happened during the week on a slip of paper and place it in a large glass vase. Throughout the week, I find myself thinking about things that happen and wondering if they will make it into the jar.

I have also had weeks from hell. This is a great way to bring positive affirmations into your life while providing uplifting closure to those rough weeks and setting your attitude right for the upcoming week. Also, it's fun to see the jar fill up! At the end of the year, I will have a whole jar of great things that happened to remind me how blessed my life is. On January 1 each year, I start all over again. I found this simple exercise doable. It is helping me live a life of gratitude, nourishing my emotional and spiritual needs, and allowing all the other aspects of my well-being to blossom.

Enough Is Enough

Somehow, I had gotten myself into way too many activities. I felt like an octopus and had eight arms all doing different things. Night after night, I was at one activity or another, and it got to a point where I was stretched so thin that I didn't enjoy any of it. My life was a haphazard grab bag of activities that normally would be beneficial and fun, but they only served to exacerbate my issues and imbalance. It was exhausting, and the physical component of my well-being suffered. I was not in a good place emotionally because the overload was too much for my brain to handle. Sadly, there were some activities I'm sure I would have enjoyed but being involved in so many detracted from the experiences each had to offer. Each of these activities was nothing more than a Band-Aid covering deeper wounds. I had cancer, and I was trying to forget it, but I needed to deal with the fact that cancer had happened—and it had changed me.

It Could Always Be Worse

Some of the support groups and spiritual sessions were full of people like me who felt lost or broken. While the sum of all my experiences and setbacks was hard for me, others have had even more challenging obstacles. As I talked to others about their stories, I came to realize that what I went through, though traumatic and awful, could have been even worse. There is always a bigger fish. Fortunately for me and those close to me, my cancer story had a happy ending. For some, cancer will always be a way of life. It is often a chronic condition that is full of remissions and recurrences. Others would love the opportunity to find their way through this world of recovery, but unfortunately, they succumb to the disease and never get the chance.

The Answer Has Always Been There

Through my experiences, I have learned two things that changed my recovery from frustration to optimism:

1. I can only find myself, by myself, and no one else can do it for me.
2. The moment I stopped trying so hard to heal is when I finally started to heal.

As survivors, we come out of our cancers often looking to external sources to find peace instead of looking in the most difficult place: our own hearts and minds. The answers we find can be scary, and we might discover truths we don't want to hear. We have been closed off to ourselves for so long, existing in survival mode, that confidence and self-esteem have plummeted. I could not discover who this new "post-cancer me" is until I removed the image I had of the perfect "pre-cancer" me off the pedestal and accepted that version of me was gone. Allowing myself to believe in the possibility that the post-cancer me had much to offer, without the need of external distractions, was when I could discover who I was.

Lessons Learned

1. It's OK to feel lost. Finding yourself again after a trauma can, in and of itself, be traumatic. Healing can make us feel worse before we feel better; the protective walls built up to keep from being vulnerable must be broken down. This can be hard to face. Stay with it—you are healing!
2. Try using these six areas of balanced well-being to do a self-evaluation. Identify areas of strength as well as areas you would

like to improve. Then seek enriching activities and practices that can bring them into balance.

3. Be willing to explore and try something totally of your wheelhouse. Limit yourself by finding one or two things you love to do and focusing on them. My experiences can serve as a lesson that too much can only serve to muddy the waters of recovery and healing.

4. Trust your instincts. You will know when something positively impacts you. Run with it and explore all it can offer. Maybe it will be a counselor, a shaman, an art class, or just connecting with nature. It can be anything.

5. Remember, healing comes from within. If external sources help, it is because you have found a way to internalize them and make them work for you!

6. Finally, accept who you are and where you are on this journey. When I embraced that I was changed by cancer, chemo, and all that had happened, I transformed from simply surviving and existing, into a victorious woman who can do anything. That is when you will soar!

CHAPTER 13B: JOHN

Stopping the Cycle

Being a Team Player

I think everyone can look back at new things they have tried and wonder, *What was I thinking?* When Sherri went from treatment into recovery, a whole new quest of self-discovery began. Neither of us knew how hard it was going to be. Honestly, it is ongoing. For my part, I was fully ready to go from caregiving to cheerleader, helping Sherri get her body back to its normal self. Not in a million years did I anticipate taking part in some of the activities and events she signed us up for. The greatest challenge was forgetting that these things were for her—not me. What follows are some curious stops Sherri took me to on her journey. Your caregiving journey is not over when your loved one is discharged from treatment. Recovery is quite a ride.

Do Not Get in the Way

When it became clear that Sherri was regaining her strength, her desire to push her mind and body increased. At the time, my role was to encourage and support. Seeing her reclaim independence and be active again was awesome. Hell, I just wanted to get out of her way! This girl was bound and determined to prove to the world and herself that she was back. Subsequently, she dove headfirst back into a busy, active life. Not knowing some of that crazy shit she was going to drag me into, along I went!

Driving Miss Daisy

At first, my role was just to be a chauffeur. She wanted to start getting involved in various activities, but she was leery of navigating the highways by herself. The thought of her out on the interstate and navigating downtown was worrisome. Navigating skills were never her strength, and inevitably, I would get a tearful call saying she was lost—even though she was using

GPS. It was just easier to take on the role of chauffeur, but inevitably, that meant I would also be participating in her newfound adventures.

Recognizing and Responding to a Pattern

The new format we would follow for the next two and a half years was to try something new, jump right into yet another activity, class, or session, and come away with some successes, some failures, and some downright anger. Even though I could see the overload on her, my support remained strong for everything she wanted to try. My theory was simple: Sherri wanted to leave cancer in the rearview mirror, but she was trying too hard and would not stop. Between classes, volunteering, starting her massage practice, and working full-time, she was consumed.

The pattern was becoming desperate. Sherri was so determined to prove she was normal, but since most of the things she signed up for did not provide affirmation, she simply added more to her plate. As a caregiver, I was caught up in this as well, and it was taking a toll. I was frustrated, and I wanted to get back into doing things for myself too. I could see it was time to step in and act, for both our sakes. If I was going to be an effective caregiver for Sherri, I had to have some sort of self-fulfillment too. I needed to be willing to do the hard thing. It was time for an intervention—one that was necessary for both of us to experience joy again.

A Reckoning: Stopping the Vicious Circle

How should I do this? How should I tell Sherri that her plan is failing? Maybe not failing, but it certainly was not coming to the fruition she had hoped for. She was headed for a hard crash if she did not stop. I mulled over this for a couple of weeks. What finally made it obvious that intervention was necessary was when she began to physically decline.

On the occasional evening Sherri was home, she was visibly becoming more fatigued earlier and earlier. The stress she had created for herself was spilling into our home life. I had to do more to help her get through it, which was becoming a source of my own stress. I felt like I was walking on eggshells around her, and it was exhausting for me. The final straw was that she was getting ready to sign up for yet another eight-week series of painting classes. Seeing where this was going, it was time to intervene. I was at my wit's end watching Sherri reach her own wit's end. I was fearful she would get herself sick all over again.

I said. "Do you think that maybe you just are doing too much?"

She asked what I meant, and I proceeded to run through the laundry list of things she was trying to do all at once.

She froze, looked at me for a moment, and said, "You're right." I was not prepared for what happened next. She then proceeded, at a diligent pace, to pack up all her art supplies. She put away her paper, pencils, paint, and paintbrushes. In a matter of minutes, everything was off the table and neatly tucked away on a shelf. Ugh, I wanted to crawl under a rock. I felt like I had crushed her world. I never intended for her to give up everything she was doing. That was not the desired outcome, but she had made her mind up, and once that happens, it just happens.

I could not tell at first, but she really was not upset with me. Sherri would have felt like a failure if she had quit on her own. Pointing out that she was way too busy gave her a welcome reprieve and a way out from under all the strain. Sherri accepted that she was involved in way too much and realized cutting back was OK. She could allow herself to slow down and reset. This brought a rush of relief for me as well.

Since Then

I have learned a great deal on this continuously evolving pathway to recovery. Though undying support is the rule, sometimes that support means having difficult conversations. Confrontation is not fun. Intervention to change someone else's behavior is uncomfortable and unpleasant, but it may be necessary.

On a lighter note, throughout this part of the recovery journey, an unexpected development was that I discovered some things about myself too. Being open to new things, strange practices, and crazy rituals was eye-opening and enjoyable. In fact, I have adopted some of them. I enjoy yoga and meditation, and Sherri and I are now both certified yoga instructors! These practices have helped me move on as well.

Takeaways

1. Intervention is hard, but in some cases, it is necessary. Sometimes you lead, sometimes you get out of the way, and sometimes you need to get back *in* the way.

2. Do not be a bystander and watch your loved one go down paths that will only set them up for failure. I have no regrets stepping in and telling Sherri she was in over her head doing all those activities. Today, she thrives in many ways because of it.

3. What can I say? Be open-minded about new things. Along the way, you might discover things you never knew about yourself.

4. As caregivers, we cannot ignore that we need self-fulfillment too. By taking the steps to help Sherri, I was able to regain some of my own life.

CHAPTER 14: JOHN

I Wanna Talk about Me!

Taking Care of the Caregiver

"All I ask is that you give 110 percent. All I ask for is all you have." Typically, we hear these phrases in the sports world, but they also belong in "Caregiving 101."

Everything has been about Sherri. From the first cough and all through recovery, any interests, hobbies, or anything in my life that was just for me had to stop. In that moment when we got the diagnosis, I gave up everything; it was necessary and the absolute right thing to do, but it took some getting used to.

When she found herself struggling in recovery, Sherri learned she needed to address the six major components of a well-balanced person. I get it. For her to regain any semblance of a normal life, she needed to find balance in all those areas, but what about me as a caregiver? How do I take care of myself so that I can be the best caregiver for her and not lose myself in the process?

I caught myself more than a few times feeling guilty as I would wonder, *When do I get to be "me" again?* This struggle is real. One of the greatest obstacles is finding time for yourself. It would be easy for me to lecture about the importance of finding "me" time. As a caregiver, you might already have figured out that you will be so busy caregiving, working, managing the home, running errands, and so on that carving out time for yourself seems impossible and unimportant, considering everything else going on.

From "You're Cured!" to "When Will This Ever End?"

When the oncologist declared Sherri cured and treatments ended, we both were elated beyond measure. We both began asking ourselves, "Now what?" Sure, we thought we would settle right back into our lives and do the things we enjoy both individually and together. I had no idea that recovering was going to be so long and demanding. I had no clue how lost and confused it would leave both of us. I often found myself feeling down or experiencing self-pity, and my head was full of questions: *Why can't Sherri just move on? Why is this so hard for her?*

Resentment is too strong a word. Frustration and impatience are better words to describe what I experienced throughout the cancer, treatments, and recovery. I never resented Sherri, but I found myself resenting the situation, especially when she was in a recovery that seemed to take forever. Hiding my feelings was easy enough. Not being able to do my own thing and have some time for myself was hard. I had no idea I would be on caregiver duty indefinitely.

Self-care is critical for the caregiver, and you must find ways to release tension, have fun, or relax. Here are some suggestions and ideas I tried. What worked for me may not be your thing, but it may help spur your own ideas. The theme is consistent: be resourceful and make some me time.

During the Battle

It cannot be overstated that self-care while your loved one is in the throes of the battle is especially important. When you are driving to and from home, work, and the hospital, you will not be thinking about how to take care of yourself physically, emotionally, or mentally. However, you may be thinking about how much you miss laughing and being out with friends—or perhaps you just miss a simpler time. If you have the added burden of living far from the hospital where treatment is administered, you have that added burden of travel, living out of a suitcase, and being away from family. You are going to need an outlet.

Sherri addressed six key areas of a well-balanced person from a patient's perspective. It's equally important to explore these as a caregiver. The physical, mental, emotional, social, spiritual, and environmental components need to be balanced for us to function optimally for ourselves and those we care for. These six components were not part of my thought process at the time. All I could focus on was the sorts of things I could do for myself in the limited time I had. Of course, it would have been better balanced if I had been aware of the six components.

Physical

The physical was the most doable and what I most enjoyed. When Sherri was asleep or resting, I could make quick trips to the gym or go for a walk or a jog. The staff had made it possible for me to use the OSU student rec center during inpatient stays. This was a welcome release of stress and anxiety. The small act of setting me up with passes to the rec center went a long way toward keeping me sane while staying at the hospital. If that is not an option, get out and walk or go for a jog. Just move.

Mental

I was mentally taxed by managing my teaching, coaching, reading up on Sherri's treatments and complications, and managing our day-to-day personal affairs. I tried to read books, but I never could focus for long. I stayed focused on the tasks at hand, and out of fear of letting my guard down, I never strayed. Meditation allowed me to put things in perspective and focus on the tasks at hand.

Finding my Zen is not something I have ever been able to do easily, but with practice, it was helped me throughout Sherri's battle. I had to sit in the hospital room for long stretches, often for days in a row. I downloaded an app and began learning to meditate.

I have an overactive mind that sometimes doesn't stop. During that year from hell, it interfered with sleep. I was running on empty, and ultimately my body just hit a wall. Meditation served me well both mentally and emotionally. I still practice meditation today, and it helps in all aspects of my life. Maybe you like podcasts or reading...finding those things that will keep your mind alive and stimulated as well as bring you some peace.

Social

I missed being able to do activities I used to enjoy with others: play golf, grab a beer, or watch a game. My social interactions were truly limited to Sherri, the hospital staff, and my coworkers. I was not equipped to address this component outside of my time with Sherri. What helped was planning "dinner dates" in the hospital room or long walks with Sherri and "Ivy." These had to suffice as my social interactions.

If you can't leave your loved one alone yet, reach out to family or close friends who can come over and give you a break from caregiving. If you have kids at home, ask family or trusted friends to give you a couple of hours and babysit. Getting out with a friend for a bit to socialize can do wonders to reset.

Once your loved one has regained their strength and independence, it is OK for you to start regaining your independence as well. Rediscover the things you used to do and enjoy—just for yourself. It may be quite gradual at first, but continue to develop your own interests for optimal health and well-being. You may feel some guilt at not being present with your loved one around the clock, but if you allow your own health and well-being to slide, you have accomplished nothing.

Spiritual

Our church attendance became sparse. Sherri could not attend, and I was not going to leave her alone for too long. Our pastor made regular visits to see us at the hospital. The hospital had volunteers to administer Communion and pray with us. This is one area that is personal and specific to you. Explore your own spiritual needs and ways to meet them. I found I did not need to be at church to pray, read, and contemplate my faith.

Journaling was never my thing. While many people can confide in a family member or close friend, others may not have that luxury. Keeping a journal to record the timeline of events along with the accompanying emotions is a healthy way to vent feelings that may otherwise accumulate, become destructive, and affect your coping abilities. For me, this was an extension of keeping my daily calendar up to date, which I find therapeutic since I am hell-bent on being organized. The physical act of writing is an outlet of sorts, and you will connect with your feelings better as you write. I am list maker, and my journaling started out in my monthly planner. I just recorded exactly what happened each day of Sherri's ordeal. Once the diagnosis came down, I found myself bottling up my fears and concerns to keep from adding to Sherri's stress. I began to take notes about what I was thinking and feeling, especially in times of high anxiety. I only need to see what happened on a specific day, like the day of one of her surgeries, to instantly recall the day and the emotions.

As time passes, some of that will fade. My journal was a major source for my contributions in this book.

Emotional

I sort of put my emotions in a box and put it on a shelf. The walls went up. I convinced myself I needed to be solid as a rock and that Sherri did not need her caregiver losing it. I didn't ask for help; it didn't even occur to me. Sure, there were people I could have talked to, but I did not take advantage. Maybe it was my male ego wanting to look strong that prevented me, but I wish I had sought out a friend to consistently talk to. Ask for help.

When your loved one is in and out of the hospital or has extended stays, seek out resources the hospital may have available for caregivers. You will need to initiate it since the patient is the number one priority. Unless you ask, you may not be openly offered these opportunities. Many hospitals are starting to get more in tune with the importance of supporting caregivers. Hospitals realize the patient's network of caregivers is an important part of patient healing.

Environmental

Get outside. Go to the park and hike a short trail. Take the dog on a walk. Heck, even mowing the lawn would count. I went outside any chance I could, especially to get a break from the hospital. In many ways, addressing the environmental component is overlooked, but it can improve the other five! For you, it might be going to a park, perusing a library or museum, or anything else that gives you a respite from being on duty 24/7.

Mapping Your Unique Journey

The caregiver journey is as unique as a patient or survivor journey; it is also unique to the individual. That being said, I fully realize that I present a perspective from that of a middle-aged man whose children have all grown, and my caregiving was for Sherri, who is also my age. I don't have all the answers. Every caregiver has their own unique situations and challenges. Caregiving for my wife was an entirely different scenario than caring for a sick child, an elderly family member, or being a caregiver with children still at home. While we all face unique challenges, we all share the same need to cut ourselves some slack. Find a little bit of time to show yourself some love. The demands on a caregiver are many and constant. We are only human, and without self-care, we will eventually fall. You need to take care of yourself.

Takeaways

1. Self-care matters. You will be no good to the one you are caring for if you become so tired, worn down, and stressed that you become ill. How can you expect to be the best caregiver if you allow yourself to wear down mentally, physically, and emotionally?
2. Self-care is important all through the process—not just during diagnosis and treatment. Recovery can be long, demanding, and exasperating. When possible, rekindle your hobbies and social life—even if just occasionally.
3. You will be torn between doing even the smallest thing for yourself and remaining on duty as caregiver. You may experience guilt for wanting to do something for yourself. Do it anyway. A little short-term guilt is better than long-term resentment of your loved one.
4. Journal some form of it for your own well-being. You need a consistent place to express yourself, and this allows you to write down your deepest fears and concerns, which you might not share with others.
5. Calm the mind. I learned meditation. Whatever method you discover, just breathe!
6. My caregiving experience is not yours. What you need to do for yourself is up to you. Identify one thing in each of the component areas and create some self-care opportunities.

CHAPTER 15A: SHERRI

Hearing My Fight Song

Changing the Voices in My Mental Recovery

This chapter is about a transformation; positive voices were cultivated and nurtured, eventually overcoming the negative ones. Negative voices, so numerous and loud, just kept creeping out of the crevices of my mind, endlessly whispering that I could get sick again, leading me to believe a cough meant the cancer was back, or that struggling to generate words meant brain tumors. The voices sometimes seemed as if they were the narrators of a play—with my succumbing to cancer as the climax. The voices were sometimes so loud and overwhelming, and they seemed impossible to silence. It was either going to be them or me. Only I could make them stop.

Failed Attempts

Diving into dozens of activities to rediscover my life was a mistake. My expectations were always high that whatever I was involved in would solve my problems. Instead of enjoying anything for just the experience, I went in guns-a-blazin' with the intent that said activity was going to be the catalyst in my recovery and the key to discovering a new and improved me! Of course, it was naturally expected that the leaders of the group would have all the answers. And, of course, they did not.

Time after time, I went in with high hopes—only to walk away disheartened, the voices of negativity all the louder. Other participants joyously chatted while waiting for class to start; on and on they talked about their "grand spiritual journeys" to self-discovery. I was absolutely certain a two-by-four of revelation would hit me upside the head and say, "Hey! This is who the new you is supposed to be—and this is what you are now going to do." Or maybe someone was going to give me a brochure with steps A, B and C all smartly written out and say, "Contact our help desk anytime!" And, when nothing went as planned, I could hear those awful voices again.

They Aren't Going Anywhere

The root of the problem was right in front of me the whole time. I was never going to silence all that negativity just by staying busy and overly involved. Trying to utilize only external sources turned out to be a failed plan.

While expressing my frustrations about being overwhelmed, a good friend made the simplest, most common-sense analogy. Apparently, as she saw it, I was trying to remove the "dandelions in my yard" by just trying to pull off their heads. I needed to look much deeper. This sense of being lost and scared would keep coming back until I was able to remove the roots of the problem. Blink! The lights came on.

To get out of this deep hole, something within had to change. Those voices are never going to stop or change their tune. I live with the fact that they still hide in those crevices, resurfacing from time to time. The answer to squelching them lies in awakening new, more positive, and much louder messages. After easing up on my involvement in "stuff," my mind was free, and I didn't have to try so hard. I wish I could tell you how it happened, or the very moment it happened, but I cannot. There was not a truly aha moment and certainly no two-by-four to the head, but finally, the positive side started to win. If you really want to change, stop trying so hard.

Acceptance

To overcome the doubt running through my mind, I had to accept the realities of my life. Acceptance that there had been a terrible event, something that happened to me, and it changed me. Acceptance too, that not only was there change, but part of the impact resulted in some short-term and long-term limitations. I will never be the exact person I was before cancer. Stop judging and start accepting. Embrace the me who cancer happened to and not the cancer girl who was defined by it. Knowing and accepting these new realities made a huge difference in drowning out the negativity and freeing me to live again.

Stop Focusing on the Destination

When we had traveled to Europe to visit our son and his wife, we immediately noticed that the pace of life was generally slower. The people were not in a hurry all the time. People were living in the moment. It was quite clear that dinner at a restaurant was meant to be savored, and the conversation was as important as the delicious food and enjoyed by all at the table. It was not hurry and order, shovel in the food, pay the check, and get out, which was our typical pattern when dining out. People were out walking, biking, and hiking. They were truly engaged with each other. It was nothing at all like the lifestyle we were accustomed to.

Why are we not living in moments and soaking in all we can each day? This was a question we started asking ourselves. Continuous fixation on where we are going and not enjoying where we are seemed to me to be a fundamental flaw in our thinking. Where we failed is that the journey got lost. So much time was wasted focusing on the destination that life slipped by. I had been trapped in that pattern for more than a year into recovery.

I was always longing for either who I was or fixated on the vision of who I thought I was supposed to be. I was letting days, weeks, and months of my life go by while not enjoying them, victim to the triggers and negative messages that were swirling around in my head. People will often postpone their happiness until tomorrow, focusing endlessly on an end goal. Then, tomorrow becomes today, and they keep repeating the process; they never do achieve happiness. We may never be satisfied with where we are on our current journey unless we come to grips with the idea that the *journey*, not the destination, is what matters most.

Flipping My Vision

Accentuate the positive! A book by Louise Hay, *You Can Heal Your Life*, reintroduced me to positive affirmations. I have always believed that we bring back into our lives what we put out to the world. There are but twenty-four hours in the day. I can live them seeing things positively or negatively. Think of it as training myself to see the world with a different pair of glasses. Not necessarily rose-colored ones. I can still see the negative, but I actively seek the positive things going on around me. The days go by no matter how I choose to see them—why not make my days better and happier by choosing optimism? It takes practice, lots and lots of practice. But we can either get busy living or get busy dying! Every part of my well-being benefits from positive affirmations. They are now in my daily routine and part of meditation.

Instead of listening to the triggering negative thoughts of fear, sadness, and failure, I began to hear positive messages that things were going to be okay. I stopped judging so harshly and accepted myself, coming to the realization that I was more than okay. I am a strong survivor, and I was victorious over cancer! When I look in the mirror, I now see someone strong, and the scars empower me rather than serve as daunting reminders. While I cannot point to one thing for you to focus on as the end-all solution, the thing to latch onto here is that healing comes from within. Only by looking deep inside myself was transformation possible. A quote from Buddha sums it up: "Our life is shaped by our mind; we become what we think."

Lessons Learned

1. There will be voices of doubt, fear, and anxiety. Accept that truth. Acknowledging and accepting are the first step to conquering them.
2. True self-love can only come from within ourselves. We can read all the positive quotes, listen to inspirational talks, and read all the success stories and books until we are blue in the face. But those are all external things. The real work begins inside you. The important thing is to always get up and keep going!
3. Don't let a bad moment, experience, or day undo all the progress you have made. Everyone is human, and everyone must work at developing and feeding their positive self-image. People who appear to vibrant, energetic, and confident have had to work at it—just like you are. They've been practicing longer!
4. If you have overcome an illness or are currently struggling through one, you are strong! If you are a caregiver, you are strong! No matter where you are in your story, you did not quit—and you keep getting up over and over again. Celebrate that!
5. Enjoy the journey! Let go of the TGIF mindset. We often wish away the workweek. Be grateful for all the minutes every day. Amazing moments do not only happen on weekends, but we will miss them

if our hearts are only looking to the future. If we limit our focus to the destination, we miss out on many aspects in life we have been blessed with. Life is a journey—soak in every moment of it.

6. With practice, your positive voice will be shouting from the mountaintops!

CHAPTER 15B: JOHN

Planting Flowers

Helping Sherri Eliminate the Weeds

There are days when I drift off and reminisce about my experiences in life and think about the challenges I have faced, most of which are related to work. In fact, most of the difficulties were self-generated high expectations, such as the continual drive to build, maintain, and improve a successful football program. That task was enormous in my mind and consumed me for years, but then there came this obstacle; the challenge of taking care of Sherri was certainly not self-imposed, and it was not something that someone did to either of us.

My Purpose

The intention here is to give a little more common-sense advice and simple suggestions to help your loved one. Sometimes they need us, the caregivers, to apply the Band-Aid, but ultimately, only they can do the deep healing. Sometimes they need us to help them cultivate a garden full of hope and joy.

Weeds and Flowers

Years ago, growing up, we always had a large garden in the backyard. Naturally, the responsibility of taking care of the garden fell on us kids. I hated weeding! That garden got full sun all day, and lots of open dirt meant tons of dandelions, crabgrass, and some weeds that looked otherworldly.

When we protested, our parents always said, "If you want to eat, then get out there and get that garden weeded!"

Recently, this memory was brought back to life while attending a meditation class at our local yoga studio. The instructor was telling a story about removing the bad things that have happened to us and letting them go so we can move on and allow more positivity into our thoughts and lives.

The story was simple, and apparently any gardener knows this. If you want to remove the weeds from your garden, it is a lot easier to plant flowers than continuously having to keep pulling the weeds out by hand. What an intriguing concept! Makes sense that the mass planting of flowers would keep direct sunlight off the soil, preventing the germination of weeds. The instructor also said that flowers will use up the water and nutrients weeds normally require, thereby depriving the weeds. In other words, the flowers will starve the weeds, leaving you with a healthy, relatively weed-free garden that also looks beautiful.

Revelation! This made great sense, and I could instantly see the metaphor at work. Most of us can deal with negativity and unfortunate events because we have a support system around us. That, and perhaps the sum of our life experiences, has hardwired us in a way that we can respond and forge ahead. Sherri was that person, but when the cancer hit, it completely rocked her world. She began to question whether everything she ever did to live a healthy lifestyle even mattered. Repeatedly, she would ask, "Why me?" She questioned her own existence and everything she knew and believed about health and preventing illness. Metaphorically, the weeds began to grow and take over in the garden of her mind and heart.

Plant Flowers, John!

When I thought about it, it occurred to me that I already was doing this! Encouragement, support, celebrations, being a guiding voice—I have been planting flowers since the day the first cough occurred. Following my caregiver instincts all along was just like planting flowers. When Sherri was sick, it was the hugs, hand-holding, and basically being there. In recovery, it was helping her function at home, encouraging her reengagement with life, going to appointments, and providing reassurance that she was getting better.

Today, much less is required of me. Sherri is strong and vibrant now; she is an independent, active woman. The flowers I plant now are saying "I love you" often and reminding her that she is A-OK—even when the shadows in the back of her mind creep out. Helping her discover her wellness journey and rekindle things she is passionate about are the flowers I plant today. Okay, Mom and Dad, why on earth did we *not* plant flowers back in the day?

If Only We had a Blazed Trail for Cancer and Recovery

Sometimes, all it takes from a caregiver is a calming voice of reason and logic. Sometimes, you just need to be the path your loved one needs to follow. Recently, we went on a hiking vacation with our sons in North Carolina. We spent a few days in a quaint cottage near the mountains, just outside of Asheville, and it was a great trip. We were having a great time on a five-mile hike, but did we check the weather? Uh, no. That was the one thing we did not do that day, and it proved to be a big mistake. We plotted our course to the trailhead and drove early on a beautiful sunny morning. Off we went, not realizing that a powerful storm was tracking our way. We made it to the top of the trail and noticed a chilly breeze and darkening skies.

As we began to descend the mountain, Mother Nature unleashed her fury on us. We had never been out in a storm like that without access to shelter. Brutal winds and blinding sheets of rain pelted us. Lightning was flashing everywhere, and then it hit a tree not too far away—and the tree came crashing down. This went on for the entire three miles remaining to get back down to the trailhead. The rain was coming down so hard that the trails were being washed out from under us. Rivers of mud and debris were flowing down and across the path. At times, we had to climb and scramble on the steep slopes to find our course because the path had been washed away. Quite a harrowing experience! When we finally got to the bottom of the trail, the rain subsided—and the sun soon came back out. It was utterly unreal.

The message here for caregivers is fitting. Not having a marked path on a hike can be concerning. Getting lost in the wilderness is certainly not a good idea. In that harrowing downhill race to get out of that storm, I realized how important a blazed trail really is. As caregivers, we *are* the trailblazers. And when our loved ones are mired in fear and feel lost in a driving storm, we are the ones who can provide them a way back to the main road.

Planting Something a Little Different: Reverse Psychology

Sometimes the pathways provided were just a reassuring word or two. Other times, if she was reaching the point of panic, I flipped the situation and said, "Well, if you really are that worried, maybe we should make an appointment. They can do blood tests and take a scan."

She would say, "Oh, no. I don't want to do that. I don't think it is anything that bad." She admitted and told herself she was okay.

I do not make a big deal of it. I just change the subject and talk about something else. I see myself as the rudder on a sailing ship. Every now and then, she lets go of the steering wheel and drifts off course. I just correct the rudder a bit and encourage her with a suggestion or a prod to grab back on and steer the ship on its course.

Takeaway

1. Get planting! That's it.

CHAPTER 16

Learning to Thrive on the Other Side

Time Keeps on Tickin'

Invisible and fleeting, time often seems to slip by so fast, and at other times, we feel stuck in slow motion. The age-old mystery as to why the best times of our lives go by so fast is almost eclipsed by contemplating why the worst events in our lives, especially while we are experiencing them, seem to never end. This healing and recovering? It is going to take time more than you want it to.

There are plenty of self-help professionals out there with advice on the stages of cancer recovery. We have listened to several, and their messages are good, but not one of them can fast-forward your recovery. There is no remote-control device out there that allows you to skip ahead to the "healed you." That window of time is uniquely yours, and only you can work through it.

The long-term goal is healing rather than a quick fix. This is accomplished by learning the lessons only time can offer. Acknowledging that it will take time, through trial and error, you and your caregivers will find your way. We could not truly begin to thrive until we discovered and came to grips with the fact that recovery is ongoing. As you find your own way—and we cannot stress this enough—please be kind to yourselves.

Why Not Me?

Have you ever had one of those dreams where you were running from something horrible, like a monster or a demon? You woke up suddenly and though you may not have recalled the dream exactly, you know you were scared out of your wits! For many of us, that dream is our reality as we continually run scared from the monster of cancer. We carry high levels of insecurity, sometimes anger, and perhaps even resentment. Often, we ask the same daily questions: Why me? Why now? What caused this? What did I do to deserve this?

We both replayed that dream for weeks, even months, after treatment stopped. The incredible fear of cancer returning dominated our lives for what felt like an eternity. We both were riding waves of turbulent emotions and were truly stuck in the mud. When talking with others who are on or have traveled this journey, it seems everyone can connect with this nightmare on some level.

Finally, that day came when the patient stopped being a patient. She turned to face the demons head-on, just as if fighting the cancer itself again. Instead of asking "Why me?" the question changed to "Why not me?" Cancer was not selective; it was a random thing that happened to me, like it could happen to anyone else. We both accepted what happened, stopped questioning the why and how it occurred, and acknowledged that it happened. We determined that it was just a chapter in our lives and not some new definition of who we are. Today, finally we are no longer the patient and caregiver. We are just Sherri and John.

EPILOGUE

A Real Connection

The idea for this book was born in the hospital during Sherri's final stay before she was discharged for the last time. We were alone and reliving the saga of the past twelve incredible months of our lives. In the discussion, we both agreed that, for whatever reason, cancer happened. It wasn't fair, and it wasn't right, but it happened. And it happened to us. We wanted to move on, but we never wanted to forget. At the time, the emotions were raw, and we were different, changed forever down to our very core. But with time, those changes and emotions diminished, and the lessons we wanted to remember, which had been so ingrained in our minds early on, were forgotten. Yet, the memories we wanted to forget, we could not let go of. We decided to document our story, mostly for our own healing. In talking with others, we realized our story is more common than it is unique; many others have experienced the frustrations of trying to navigate their way like us. And it is not only the survivors; it is also the caregivers.

Unexpectedly, our story evolved into something more. We wanted to reach out to the ever-growing number of people who are also trying to navigate this word of recovery. Everyone talks about how cancer changed them, but the bigger picture was the change in their relationships to others, especially their loved ones and caregivers. We felt strongly that the voices of the survivor and the caregiver needed to be heard equally.

We had no idea how difficult writing this narrative would be. Digging out the old calendars, journals, and medical documents required revisiting key moments on the timeline, prompting us to relive all those memories. Inevitably, we were spiraling back down into that rabbit hole and rediscovering how real and raw those days still are. If we are experiencing these emotions, even after some time has passed, surely others are too!

We didn't want to write just a memoir. Since this piece had to be much more, we focused on more than the cancer experience. We tried to deal with questions of "Now what?" and "Where do we go from here?"

Finding our way out of that abyss will always live in our memories as some of the hardest times of our lives. While we certainly do not claim to have all the answers, we offer familiar and experienced voices to you, our fellow survivors and caregivers. You are not alone. What you are feeling is normal, and if you stumble and fall, you have it within yourself to get back up.

RESOURCES FOR SURVIVORS AND CAREGIVERS

In doing the research for this book, our eyes were opened to many resources that are available to patients and caregivers. Unfortunately, during treatment, we were not aware of all the programs that existed. We were so zoned in on the fight that we didn't think to the seek outside help beyond the medical world. Since the cancer world was new to us, we didn't know what we didn't know—and we had no idea what to even ask. Here are several resources that we hope will help you navigate the world of cancer and recovery.

General Resources

* Denotes One-on-one support provided
American Cancer Society
https://www.cancer.org/
Many resources and support services for patients and caregivers through
    cancer and beyond.

*Cancare
https://cancare.org/
Whether you need support or want to give it. Cancer survivors and
    caregivers are matched with others who have similar struggles. Their
    motto is "No one should endure cancer alone."

Cancer 101
https://cancer101.org/
Their mission statement sums it up: "To empower, inform and engage
    patients and their caregivers to take control over their diagnosis,
    navigate the cancer journey, and partner with their health care team to
    make informed decisions."

Cancer Care
https://www.cancercare.org/tagged/post-treatment_survivorship

Provides free, professional online support services for people who have completed cancer treatment and additional resources.

Cancer and Careers:
https://www.cancerandcareers.org/en
Worth a look for anyone managing cancer and life. Life-managing tools to keep organized. Many aspects of cancer and the workplace during treatment and returning to work.

*Cancer Hope Network
https://www.cancerhopenetwork.org/
Instill hope and make a positive difference through one-on-one support to all people impacted by cancer—from diagnosis through survivorship.

Cancer.Net
https://www.cancer.net/
Survivorship section provides general resources and helpful information for cancer survivors of all ages on a wide range of topics.

*Cancer Support Community
https://www.cancersupportcommunity.org/
Provides professional, educational, and community support to patients and caregivers. Holds to the belief no one should face cancer alone.

Cancer Treatment centers of America (CTCA)
Cancercenter.com

Cancer Fighters
https://www.cancerfighter.com/get-support/cancer-support-group/

Complete Resource List Encompassing a Wide Variety of Helpful Agencies

*Imerman Angels
https://imermanangels.org/
The mission statement of Imerman Angels' is to provide comfort and understanding for all cancer fighters, survivors, previvors, and caregivers

through a personalized, one-on-one connection with someone who has been there.

Livestrong Foundation
https://www.livestrong.org/
Their goal is to put cancer survivors and their families first. They provide resources for emotional, physical, and practical challenges.

National Cancer Institute
NCI Office of Cancer Survivorship
https://cancercontrol.cancer.gov/ocs/
Focuses on understanding and supporting the unique needs of the cancer survivor and caregiver.

National Coalition for Cancer Survivorship
https://www.canceradvocacy.org/resources/
Free Cancer Survival Toolkit with modules about handling the challenges encountered when facing cancer.

*People Living with Cancer (PLWC)
https://www.uicc.org/membership/people-living-cancer-plwc
If you want to give back or need support, consider "Cancer Buddies" who provide support and understanding to new cancer patients and caregivers. Sometimes the best treatment is just talking to someone who has been there.

Pregnant with Cancer Network
https://hopefortwo.org/
Women diagnosed with cancer while pregnant connect with other women who have experienced a similar cancer diagnosis.

The Susan G. Komen Race for the Cure
https://ww5.komen.org/
Provides support through diagnosis treatment and survival as well as financial assistance.

Insurance and Financial Guidance

Cancer Financial Coalition Assistance
https://www.cancerfac.org/
Offers resources for financial and practical help such as housecleaning and
other tasks.

Patient Advocate Foundation
https://www.patientadvocate.org/
Financial aid and insurance guidance removing obstacles to quality cancer
care.

Caregiver-Specific Resources

Cancer Treatment Centers of America (CTCA) and Cancer Fighters
https://www.cancerfighter.com/get-support/caregiver-support/
Caregivers often neglect themselves. This agency helps caregivers get the
support they need and often overlook.

Caregiver.com
https://caregiver.com/
A group that is for, about, and run by caregivers. A forum for caregivers to
connect and share resources with each other as well as support.

Help for Cancer Caregivers
https://www.helpforcancercaregivers.org/
Complete a short question for a free personal care guide to help support
your well-being.

Well Spouse Organization
https://wellspouse.org/
Resources for dealing with the unique challenges that face the caregiver.
This group advocates and addresses the needs of individuals caring for
a chronically ill and/or disabled partner/spouse.

Empowerment

Look Good Feel Better
https://lookgoodfeelbetter.org/

Learn beauty techniques to help them manage the appearance-related side effects of cancer treatment. The program includes lessons on skin and nail care, cosmetics, wigs and turbans, accessories and styling, and helping people with cancer find some normalcy in a life that is by no means normal.

Project Athena Foundation
https://projectathena.org/
To help survivors of medical and/or traumatic challenges reach new athletic goals and achieve their adventurous dreams.

Sharing Information and Coordinating Help: Communication Portals

Caring Bridge
https://www.caringbridge.org/
Online journal to share and communicate with family and friends.

Lotsa Helping Hands
https://lotsahelpinghands.com/
A central place to organize and coordinate help with meals and other help for someone in need.

Share the Care
http://www.sharethecare.org/
Improve the quality of life for anyone who needs support to reduce stress, depression, and isolation on the caregiver.

Supportful
https://www.supportful.com/
Get support for all your needs in one place. Set up fundraisers, meal plans, visiting schedules, and in-person needs within minutes.

Take Them a Meal
https://takethemameal.com/
Coordinate meals for families in need.

Note: This list is not an endorsement for these agencies. It serves informational purposes only.

ACKNOWLEDGMENTS

To Dr. Robert Baiocchi and Gretchen McNally, CNP, you are both at the top of our list. We cannot thank you enough, not just for the medical care you gave, but you gave us your hearts as well. You were always available to us, no matter the time, day or night. Your confidence gave us the confidence to make it the other side. We would not be here without you both.

To the Ohio State University Wexner Medical Center, our oncology team at the James Cancer Hospital, the entire James sixteenth-floor crew, and all the staff we encountered during our stays, we wholeheartedly thank you. For such a huge facility, you always made us feel like we were the only people being cared for. We cried (a lot at first) together and laughed together. We shared family stories with each other. You all became like a second family.

To all the countless friends who were unwavering in their support, thank you. Your love and kindness kept us going on the darkest days. We especially want to thank Kevin and Kathy. You both wrapped us in a blanket of love and supported us every step of the way. You had our backs and always knew what we needed even before we did.

To Audra, you are a mighty force to be reckoned with! Your spirit, energy, and passion for the world ignited a spark in us and validated that our story needed to be shared. You gave us the confidence to discover and use our voices.

To Cindi—our friend, colleague, and confidante—sorting through this project with you was like sitting on a couch with an old friend. You reminded us of the power of listening as well as expression with sincere honesty.

To Joan and Bob (posthumously), you were always a listening ear and always checking in to see how Sherri and I were doing. Your love and prayers made all the difference. And, Dad, we miss you still.

To Bev and Bill, founding members of the three amigos. Mom and Dad, I can never thank you enough for all the road trips to visit booming towns and beautiful lakes, and your weekly visits lightened the load for John. You always kept my spirits high. We love you!

And of course, to the boys—Nick, Beau, and Brian—and now the girls, Emily and Tori. Hopefully, we've taught you to always fight for that which is worth fighting for, and if you fall, always get back up. You were the reason to keep fighting! When I fell, you always helped me get up again! We love you all!

ABOUT THE AUTHOR

Sherri and **John Snoad** are ordinary people, unexpectedly blindsided and forever changed by an extraordinary event. As a healthcare provider for over thirty years, Sherri cared for patients during all stages of cancer, but never imagined that she herself would be diagnosed and become the patient. Her husband John never thought the skills he had spent a lifetime developing as an educator and coach would be tested as he was thrust unexpectedly into the role of caregiver. The difficult journey in navigating, and eventually finding a life after cancer is seldom talked about and serves as the inspiration for this book. Sherri and John strive to inspire those who may feel lost while trying to navigate their own labyrinth of cancer and recovery. They discovered that healing, and ultimately acceptance, could only begin from within through patience and open communication with each other. Sherri and John have not only moved on but have embraced their new normal. They are the proud parents of three adult sons and their growing families. Originally from Ohio, they now reside in sunny Florida. Living by the mantra to "not let the grass grow under their feet", you can find them somewhere in the great outdoors, hiking, enjoying the water or travelling as often as they can.

88291230R00132